Assoc. Presbytery

Act of the Associate Presbytery

concerning the doctrine of grace - wherein the said doctrine, as revealed

in the Holy Scriptures, and agreeably thereto, set forth in our confession

of faith and catechisms, is asserted and vindicated, from the errors

Assoc. Presbytery

Act of the Associate Presbytery
concerning the doctrine of grace - wherein the said doctrine, as revealed in the Holy Scriptures, and agreeably thereto, set forth in our confession of faith and catechisms, is asserted and vindicated, from the errors

ISBN/EAN: 9783337291532

Printed in Europe, USA, Canada, Australia, Japan

Cover: Foto ©Lupo / pixelio.de

More available books at **www.hansebooks.com**

A C T

OF THE

ASSOCIATE PRESBYTERY,

CONCERNING THE

Doctrine of GRACE:

WHEREIN

The said Doctrine, as revealed in the *Holy Scriptures*, and agreeably thereto, set forth in our *Confeſſion of Faith* and *Catechiſms,*

Is ASSERTED and VINDICATED,

From the *Errors* vented and publiſhed in ſome *Acts* of the *Aſſemblies* of this Church, paſſed in *Prejudice* of the ſame.

WITH

An INTRODUCTION,

Diſcovering the Riſe *and* Progreſs *of the Oppoſition to the* DOCTRINE OF GRACE, *and the* Reaſon *of paſſing and publiſhing this* Act, *in Vindication of the ſame.*

EDINBURGH:

PRINTED BY NEILL AND COMPANY.

Sold by W. LAING, Edinburgh; J. DUNCAN, Glaſgow; MORISON and SON, Perth; W. KNIGHT, Aberdeen, and R. NICOL, Dundee.

M,DCC,LXXXIX.

INTRODUCTION.

Difcovering the Rife *and* Progrefs *of the Oppofition to the* Doctrine *of* Grace, *and the* Reafons *of paffing and publifhing this* Act, *in vindication of the fame.*

OPPOSITION to the revelation of the GRACE of God, is interwoven with the corrupt nature of man. There is nothing, wherein the univerfal depravation of the human nature more evidently appears, than in defpifing and rejecting the grace of God, which bringeth falvation to all men : For, by the *plan* of falvation, as it is laid out and extended in the holy Scriptures, the greateft revenue of *glory* redounds to God ; and therefore it is the greateft evidence of *enmity* in the finner, to flight the manifold wifdom and unfpeakable love of God, that fhines therein. It would feem ftrange to one, who knew nothing of the corruption of the human nature, that any fhould refufe the choiceft bleffings, for this reafon, that they are *freely* given, and becaufe it is the will of God that they be freely received by thofe who are *wretched, miferable, poor, blind and naked :* Yet fo it is, that finners, in thefe deplorable circumftances, have, in all ages, manifefted the warmeft oppofition to the *free grace* of God through Jefus Chrift, wherever it has been revealed unto them ; and this has been the fpring of all the degeneracy and apoftafy of the Church, both under the *Old* and *New* Teftaments.

When the Lord erected the *Jews* into a National Church at mount *Sinai,* the Moral Law, as it was there publifhed, and all the Sacrifices and typical Ordinances which he inftituted among them, were full of *free grace* and mercy, and were plainly defigned to lead men off from all their own doings for life, unto the doing and dying of the glorious *Meffiah* as the only ground of their juftification, and title to eternal life : But it is obvious from Scripture, that the generality of the *Jewifh* Church contemned and rejected the *grace* of God, difplayed in the types and fhadows, promifes and prophecies of that difpenfation ; therefore the Lord *gave them up to their own hearts lufts, and they wandered in their own counfels :* And fo, before their captivity, they fell frequently into idolatry, and after it, placed the whole of their righteoufnefs in the mere outward obfervance of the Ceremonial Law, together with their own traditions, as is evident from the repeated charges laid againft the *Scribes* and *Pharifees* by our Lord, when dwelling amongft us in the days of his humiliation ; and accordingly the Spirit of God teftifies

againft

againſt the great body of the _Jewiſh_ Nation, that being _ignorant_ of God's righteouſneſs, and going about to eſtabliſh their own righteouſneſs, they _ſubmitted_ not themſelves to the righteouſneſs of God.

The ſame _legal_ ſpirit appeared very early in the _Chriſtian_ Church. The natural bias that is in the heart of man, unto juſtification by **works** of the Law, diſcovered itſelf in the tenets and opinions, which were taught and vented by the _falſe teachers_ in the very firſt age of Chriſtianity; as is manifeſt from ſeveral of the _Epiſtles_ of _Paul,_ where, in oppoſition to theſe falſe teachers, the doctrine of juſtification by the _free grace_ of God, or by _faith without the works of the Law,_ is largely inſiſted upon. And as this ſpirit of _Legaliſm_ was at the bottom of all the errors that ever infeſted the Chriſtian Church; ſo we find it runs through the whole Myſtery of Iniquity, that has been vented and maintained by _Romiſh Babylon,_ to the ruin of multitudes of precious ſouls.

When the Lord was pleaſed to bring about the Reformation of this land from _Popiſh_ darkneſs, it was by the means of preaching the goſpel-doctrine of _free grace,_ and juſtification through the imputed righteouſneſs of the Lord Jeſus Chriſt. This was the _foundation_ and _ground-work_ of the other ſteps of reformation in the worſhip, diſcipline and government of the houſe of God: The Lord's ſervants being animated by faith's views of _goſpel-grace,_ were bold and valiant in ſetting up and defending all the parts of Reformation, according to the pattern ſhewn in the Word of God: And thus _a nation was born at once, and a people brought forth in one day._

But the enemies of our Reformation, envying the flouriſhing ſtate of this Church, were indefatigable in contriving ways and means to ſully her beauty, and to bring her again under the yoke of bondage, from which ſhe had been relieved by ſuch a wonderful chain of adorable providences. Accordingly, ſeveral years after the Reformation, _Prelacy_ was introduced, and the _Arminian ſcheme,_ being hatched abroad, and calculated to exalt the powers of corrupt nature, ſoon met with a favourable reception, about the beginning of the laſt _century,_ from the _Prelatic_ party both in _Scotland_ and _England;_ who, as they were pointing plainly towards _Rome,_ ſo they embraced the _Arminian_ errors, as opening a more eaſy paſſage to that idolatrous Church. Not to ſpeak of the keenneſs, whereby _Laud's_ party in _England_ propagated this doctrine, it is well known, that the apoſtate _Prelates_ in _Scotland_ at that time were moſt warm and zealous defenders thereof; as appears not only by the ſevere ſentences paſſed by that Antichriſtian court, the _high commiſſion,_ whereof they were members, againſt many of the Lord's ſervants and people, particularly, the act of _baniſhment_ paſſed againſt that eminent ſervant of Chriſt, Mr _Samuel Rutherford,_ from his flock at _Anwoth_ to _Aberdeen,_ for writing againſt the _Arminians_ at that time; but alſo, by the juſt cenſures paſſed by that memorable Aſſembly at _Glaſgow, anno_ 1638, againſt theſe pretended _Biſhops,_ and ſome other miniſters, who were deeply involved in the ſame defection;

tion : Where, besides many grofs fcandals and immoralities, it will be found, that many of thefe men were depofed, and otherwife cenfuréd, for teaching and venting *Popifh* and *Arminian* errors ; as may be feen from the tranfactions of that Affembly, related in that excellent *Latin* hiftory, entituled, *Hiftoria motuum in regno Scotiæ.*

When the *Prelates,* who were the ftrenuous defenders of *Arminianifm,* were thus juftly cenfured in *Scotland,* they fled into *England;* where, befides their being the *firft* Authors of the *civil war,* they procured a *large Declaration* to be fent unto *Scotland,* in the *King's* name, wherein that famous *Affembly* 1638, is feverely condemned in the whole of their conduct, and particularly, for inflicting cenfure upon *Arminians.* As this paper was juftly condemned by the *Affembly* that met at *Edinburgh* 1639, and afterwards by the *Eftates* of the kingdom, as a fcandalous libel upon this Church and Nation ; fo by the Lord's bleffing upon the reformation of this Church, which he then brought about by his mighty arm, the open defenders of *Arminianifm* durft not fet up their heads, during the whole time of that reforming period, till *abjured Prelacy* was again re-impofed after the *Reftoration* of King *Charles* II.

But, although the *Arminian* doctrine had poifoned multitudes both in *Scotland* and *England,* by means of the *Popifh* and *Prelatic* party of thefe times ; yet, as the errors, held by *Arminius* and his followers, were condemned by the famous *Synod* that met at *Dort, anno* 1619, and by this Church, *anno* 1638, and by all the divines of any reputation for foundnefs, both abroad and at home ; fo, this pernicious fcheme being fo directly contrary to the Scripture-doctrine contained in the *Confeffions* of the reformed Churches, few of the more fober and ferious in thefe lands were miffed thereby : Until, at length, a more *refined,* and confequently, a more *dangerous, fcheme* of *Arminianifm* was hatched and vented in *England,* by Mr *Richard Baxter ;* which, as it came nearer to the *legal terms* that fome time before had been ufed by divines of reputed orthodoxy, in explaining of gofpel-truth ; fo it quickly fpread, like an overflowing Flood, among thofe of the *Prefbyterian* perfuafion in *England,* and gradually crept into many pulpits of *Scotland,* even after the *Revolution ;* partly out of zeal againft the real *Antinomians,* and partly by reafon of the great noife raifed by fome minifters againft the preachers of the *Doctrine of Grace,* as teachers of *Antinomianifm* : And, by this means, the doctrine of the gofpel, quickly getting the name of a *new fcheme,* became, almoft every where, evil fpoken of.

When matters with refpect to doctrine came to fo deplorable a fituation in this Church, that they who taught the abfolute freedom of the Covenant of Grace, and the unlimited Grant, that God hath made in his word, of Chrift and falvation with him, to the world of mankind, and fuch like doctrines, were branded as venting a *new fcheme* of divinity ; it is no wonder that the Church of *Scotland* fhould grow worfe and worfe, and be left, in the righteous

ous judgment of God, to an open affronting of the truth of the gofpel, and confequently of Chrift himfelf, who is the fubftance of it, by the Affembly that met *anno* 1717, when they difmiffed without cenfure a *Profeffor* of *divinity*, who had taught a fcheme of *Pelagian* and *Arminian* errors mentioned and condemned in a former *Act* of this Prefbytery. And from that time forward there is the warmeft oppofition made to the DOCTRINE OF GRACE, whenever it came upon the field, before the judicatures of this Church, whereof there are fome lamentable inftances condefcended upon in the *following Act.*

From this fhort account of the *rife* and *progrefs* of the oppofition to the DOCTRINE OF GRACE, may be gathered the great hazard and danger that this Church and land are in of being over-run with *Paganifm* and *Infidelity :* For though the Lord has been pleafed to make gofpel-light break forth in fome corners of the land, yet in many more places, the darknefs is no lefs remarkably increafed, and oppofition to the truths of the gofpel is mightily abounding ; yea the floodgates of legal and corrupt doctrine are fo wide opened, particularly by *many preachers* and *minifters* that have *lately entered* into the Church, as to threaten the utter extinguifhing of any beams of light that have been fhining amongft us.

Many are the awful *fymptoms* and evidences of the danger we are in this way. Such as (1.) The intolerable freedom that is ufed with the *holy Scriptures ;* fome denying them in bulk ; others wrefting them to their own deftruction ; and others paffing profane jefts upon them ; whereby that word is fadly verified among us, 2 Pet. iii. 3.--*There fhall come in the laft days fcoffers walking after their own lufts.* (2.) *Socinian* and *Arminian* Doctrine is now in fuch general requeft, that fome have ventured openly to recommend thefe principles, without being noticed by any of the judicatories of the Church. Mr *William Wifhart, Principal of the College of Edinburgh,* has recommended Dr *Scougal's Life of God in the foul of man,* upon which Mr *Whitefield's* experiences are founded ; a book calculated to lead off from faith in the righteoufnefs of Chrift *without* us, to a righteoufnefs *within* us, and inward *fenfations* as the ground of our pardon and acceptance before God. The faid Mr *Wifhart* has alfo recommended Dr *Whichcot's* fermons unto young minifters and ftudents ; a book that is open and plain in favours of the *Socinian* and *Arminian* fchemes. When a worthy minifter of this Church recommended the *Marrow of Modern Divinity,* a book defigned to vindicate the DOCTRINE OF GRACE, in oppofition to the *Antinomian* and *Neonomian* extremes, the Affemblies *annis* 1720 and 1722 feverely animadverted upon it : But, when a fcheme of *Arminian* and *Socinian* doctrine is now recommended, the judicatories take no manner of notice of it. Hence it follows (3.) That minifters have been encouraged to entertain their hearers with *harangues* upon moral fubjects, without ever mentioning the peculiar or fupernatural truths of Chriftianity, or fhewing the connection

that

that is between the duties of the law and promises of the gospel : And consequently, the people hear nothing from many of them, but a system of heathen philosophy intermixed with *Arminian* tenets, instead of the mysteries of the gospel; whereby multitudes have been prepared for the blind reception of that *strong delusion* at this day, whereby they have believed a lie. 4. The most part by far of all the late writings, both upon the controversy with the *Deists*, and that with the *Arians*, suppose the *Arminian* principles as granted; so that, in what is looked upon to be the *fashionable reading* of the times, whatever hand the students turn unto, they must fasten upon *Arminian* principles, as out of debate : And yet this dreadful snare is scarce, if at all, taken notice of, or warned against by the most part of those to whom the instruction of youth is now committed, nor yet by the Assemblies of this Church.

From what has been said, it will easily appear to the unprejudiced, that the ministers of the *Associate Presbytery* were bound in duty to God, and to the present and succeeding generations, to pass and publish the following *act* concerning the *Doctrine of Grace* : In regard,

1. The said doctrine has met with a great deal of *opposition* from the present judicatories, as hath been hinted above ; and therefore, when truth is controverted and opposed, it ought to be transmitted to the following generation with a solemn and peculiar *testimony* unto it.

2. The Presbytery having now, for several years, observed with regret, That *Atheism* and *Infidelity* are upon the growing hand, occasioned by the free and open passage which the judicatories have made for the spreading of *Legal* and *Arminian* doctrine; they judged it their duty, without farther delay, to mint at witnessing for these great truths, which have been so particularly condemned and opposed in their day, relating to the *Freedom of Grace*, both as to the purchase and application of redemption.

3. The Assembly 1720 and 1722, having adduced our Confession of Faith and Catechisms, to *support* the errors contained in their acts ; it is therefore necessary to vindicate these our excellent standards from the *injuries* done them by these Assemblies.

4. As the *government* of the house of Christ is an hedge to the *doctrine* (for while the purity of discipline and government according to Christ's institution is maintained, it will be an effectual check upon all the errors that may be vented in prejudice of the *doctrine of his grace ;)* so, upon the other hand, when the purity of *doctrine* is corrupted, the purity of *government* cannot long subsist; of which the present judicatories give a sad and lamentable instance : Their stated and tenacious opposition to the *Doctrine of Grace* ever since the year 1717, has opened the door to all these corruptions and defections with respect to the discipline and government of the Church, which have come to such a height at this day.

For

For thefe and the like *reafons*, the *Affociate Prefbytery* appointed a committee of their number to prepare a draught of an *act*
concerning the *Doctrine of Grace, vindicating and afferting the faid*
doctrine, as revealed in the holy Scriptures, and, agreeably thereto,
fet forth in our Confeffion of Faith and Catechifms, from the errors
vented and publifhed in fome acts of the Affemblies of this Church,
paffed in prejudice of the fame. And the faid draught having been
laid before the Prefbytery, after ferious deliberation and reafoning
thereupon, it was at a meeting of Prefbytery, at *Edinburgh, Octo-*
ber 21ft 1742, *unanimoufly approven of, enacted,* and ordered to be
publifhed. The tenor whereof follows.

N. B. In this Edition, the feveral parts of the Act are diftin-
guifhed by their refpective Titles, under Sections and Articles.
Some new Titles are added, and others are more fully expef-
fed, than in the firft Edition 1744, but what is fo added is in-
clofed in crotchets.

A C T

ACT of the ASSOCIATE PRESBYTERY, concerning the *Doctrine of Grace* :

Wherein the faid Doctrine, as revealed in the *Holy Scriptures*, and agreeably thereto, fet forth in our *Confeffion of Faith* and *Catechifms*, is afferted and vindicated from the *errors* vented and publifhed in fome *Acts* of the *Affemblies* of this Church, paffed in *prejudice* of the fame.

AT *Edinburgh*, the twenty firft day of *October*, one thoufand feven hundred and forty two years. The which day and place, the *Minifters* and *Elders*, affociate together in a prefbyterial capacity, being met in Prefbytery; and taking to their ferious confideration, that though it has been the privilege of this Church, ever fince the Reformation, to enjoy pure ftandards of *doctrine*, agreeable to the holy Scriptures; particularly, the large *Confeffion of Faith*, exhibited to the Eftates of Parliament, *anno* 1551, and by them ratified, *anno* 1560, and afterwards fworn to in the *National Covenant*, together with feveral excellent *Catechifms* expreffing the fame doctrine; as alfo the *Weftminfter* Confeffion of Faith and Catechifms, now of public authority for many years, as moft agreeable to the word of God, and in nothing contrary to the received doctrine of this Church: And that though the whole land ftands indifpenfibly bound, by the oath of God, *conftantly to adhere unto and defend* the doctrine contained in the Confeffions of this Church, as *God's undoubted truth, grounded only upon his written word;* yet there has been a manifeft *departure* from the faid purity of doctrine, as formerly profeffed in this Church and land, particularly by the *prefent judicatories* of this National Church, their tolerating and protecting the erroneous, fupporting and countenancing error, and their paffing feveral acts in prejudice of, and contrary to the doctrine of the Grace of God, contained in the forefaid Confeffions and Catechifms, agreeable to the holy Scriptures; whereby a God of truth is highly difhonoured, the gofpel perverted, the whole land involved in the guilt of perjury and apoftafy from the Lord, and confequently the falvation of multitudes of fouls manifeftly endangered : And likewife confidering, that the *Affemblies* 1720 and 1722, adduce our *Confeffion of Faith* and *Catechifms*, in *fupport* of the feveral erroneous propofitions contained in the *acts* of thefe Affemblies, relative to a book entituled, *the Marrow of Modern Divinity;* whereby a

B   blot

blot and ftain is caft upon thefe excellent ftandards, and many have been poifoned with the *legal doctrine* contained in the faid acts, and propagated through the pulpits of *Scotland*, under the mafk and covert of being agreeable to the word of God, and the forefaid ftandards :

And, whereas this Prefbytery, when they enacted and publifhed their *Act, Declaration and Teftimony, for the Doctrine, Worfhip, Government and Difcipline of the Church of* Scotland, *and againft feveral fteps of defection from the fame, both in former and prefent times,* did, upon the grounds and reafons contained in the faid *act,* condemn the errors vented by Mr *Simfon* and Mr *Campbell,* which were either not noticed at all, or but flightly cenfured by the prefent judicatories ; but, by reafon of the great variety of other matters contained in the faid *act,* and that a judicial Teftimony was then neceffary without farther delay, the Prefbytery could not, at that time, enter into fuch a particular enquiry into the feveral Acts of Affembly, that either darkened or directly impugned the Doctrine of Grace in the falvation of finners, as the importance of the fubject did require ; therefore, they now find themfelves *bound* in duty and zeal for the glory of God, the vindication of his truth, as contained in the holy Scriptures, and agreeably thereto, profeffed in the public ftandards of this Church ; as alfo for contributing what in them lies, through grace, to put a ftop to the fpreading of *legal* and *Arminian* doctrine, wherewith the whole land is like to be overflown, to the ruin of many precious fouls, who, by the Lord's blefling upon this mean of his appointment, may come to be eftablifhed in the truth as it is in *Jefus ;* and farther confidering, that all ranks are indifpenfibly obliged by folemn *Covenant,* fincerely, really, and conftantly, to endeavour, in their feveral places and callings, the prefervation of the reformed religion in the Church of *Scotland,* in Doctrine, Worfhip, Difcipline and Government ; and, in like manner, the extirpation of herefy, fchifm, and whatever fhall be found to be contrary to *found doctrine,* and the power of godlinefs ; having promifed and fworn by the *great Name of the Lord our God,* that they fhall continue in the profeffion and obedience of the forefaid religion, particularly, (as in the Acknowledgment of Sins, and Engagement to Duties) againft the errors vented by the *Independents, Antinomians, Arminians, Socinians, Sceptics* and *Eraftians,* to which may be added *Neonomians :* THEREFORE, for the above and other weighty reafons, the *Affociate Prefbytery* did, and hereby do, judge it their duty according to the powers given them by the *Lord Jefus Chrift,* as a judicatory of his houfe, to affert the truth from the holy Scriptures, and our ftandards of doctrine, concerning the *free grace* of God, in the falvation of mankind loft ; in oppofition to the corrupt doctrine vented in fome *acts* of Affemblies, darkening and enervating the fame. And to this they reckon themfelves the more warranted and obliged, in regard that the falvation of finners is manifeftly endangered, by errors and miftakes anent the *nature of faith* and *God's gift* of eternal life unto the us, *complete satisfaction* of the glorious Surety, the *absolute Freedom* of the Covenant of Grace, and other important doctrines which are opposed and subverted by the Acts of Assembly after-mentioned.

SECTION I. [Concerning the injuries done to the Doctrine of Grace, by the Assembly 1717.]

ALTHOUGH the judicatories shewed such lenity towards Mr *Simson*, that much of the time of three several Assemblies, *annis* 1715, 1716, 1717, was spent in labouring to *screen* him from just censure, notwithstanding his having vented such dangerous errors, as sap the very foundation of all revealed religion; yet, when the doctrine comes upon the field, which tends to advance the *freedom of grace*, in opposition to man's natural powers of performing that which is spiritually good, it meets with a *condemnatory* sentence at once. For the Assembly that met *anno* 1717, that same day in which they dismissed the process against Professor *Simson* in such a superficial manner, they condemn in the strongest terms, the following proposition advanced by the Presbytery of *Auchterarder*, viz. *That it is not found and orthodox to teach, That we must forsake sin, in order to our coming to Christ, and inflating us in covenant with God;* for, the General Assembly " declare their " *abhorrence* of the foresaid proposition, as *unsound* and most *de-* " *testable.*" Act 10. Assem. 1717.

The Presbytery of *Auchterarder* were at that time endeavouring to put a stop in their bounds, to the spreading of *Arminian* and *Baxterian* doctrine, which was then vented in many places of the kingdom; and therefore, they agreed on some propositions, anent the *freedom of grace*, whereof the above was one, expressing the sense and meaning of our *Confession* in opposition to *legal* doctrine; and resolved to require satisfaction of young men, as to these points, before they should be licensed by them, in order to know their soundness anent the doctrine professed in the Church of *Scotland:* Yet, the Assembly did not only severely censure the conduct of that Presbytery, but condemn the above proposition in the foresaid manner; and this they did, even *before* calling that Presbytery, and hearing what they had to offer in support thereof: And having condemned it, they then ordered that Presbytery to compear before the *Commission* of Assembly in *August* thereafter, and give an account of what they meant by the above proposition. Accordingly, by act 8. 1718, it appears that the said Presbytery of *Auchterarder* compeared before the Commission, and satisfied them as to their meaning; notwithstanding whereof " The Com- " mission did admonish them, and discharged them to use that ex- " pression in time coming; and the brethren of *Auchterarder* did " engage to observe this their prohibition. The General Assem- " bly approves of the actings of the said Commission in this mat- " ter, and, for the vindication of the brethren of the Presbytery " of

" of *Auchterarder*, they appointed thefe prefents to be printed
" among their public acts."

The *Affociate Prefbytery* cannot but with regret obferve the manifeft and glaring partiality of the judicatories for many years paft, with refpect unto *Doctrine:* Shewing their difpleafure, in feveral inftances, againft thofe who vented or publifhed any thing in fupport of the *Scripture Doctrine,* concerning the *freedom of Grace,* in oppofition to the *Neonomian* fcheme ; and, upon the other hand, fcreening and protecting thofe, who have vented opinions and tenets evidently favouring *legal* and *Arminian* doctrine : And, as this has paved the way for the other defections that prefently prevail ; fo it is error in *Doctrine,* corruption in Difcipline, and tyranny in Government, wherewith the *prefent judicatories* are juftly loaded, that has now rendered communion with them moft unfafe for any that would defire to cleave to the reformed and covenanted principles of the Church of *Scotland.* Was there any thing like an equal warmth fhewn againft any, or all the errors vented by Mr *Simfon,* as in the above cafe ? No, the Affembly 1717, are at a deal of pains in their *act* to palliate and excufe them ; the worft they fay of them is, that they are " expreffions that bear, and are " ufed by adverfaries in a bad and unfound fenfe." But, when the above propofition comes upon the field,—although it has a manifeft tendency to advance the *freedom of Grace* in the application as well as the purchafe of Redemption, and was levelled againft the *legal* doctrine of the times ; yet the Affembly declare their *abhorrence* of it, as *unfound and moft deteftable.*

Now, if this propofition is to be abhorred, as *unfound* and *moft deteftable,* namely, *That it is not found and orthodox to teach, that we muft forfake fin in order to our coming to Chrift, and inflating us in covenant with God;* then, according to that act of Affembly, it would be found doctrine to teach, *That a finner muft forfake his fin, in order to his coming to Chrift ;* or, which is the fame thing, that it is a *man's duty* to forfake his fin *in order* to his coming to Chrift, but this is evidently contrary to Scripture : For,

(1.) Although it is the unqueftionable duty of the creature to forfake and abandon whatever is forbidden by the law of his Creator ; yet, fince life and immortality are brought to light by the gofpel, the law binds to the obfervation of that *order* and *connection of duties* which is laid out in the *word of grace ;* and it is plain that the *firft and leading duty,* required in the law, upon the revelation of the grace of God in the promife of the gofpel, is, *to believe that report;* for, *without faith it is impoffible to pleafe* God, *Heb.* xi. 6. *He that believeth on the Son hath everlafting life; he that believeth not the Son fhall not fee life, but the wrath of God abideth on him,* John iii. 36. Hence it follows, that according to Scripture, every act of the foul, as performed by a perfon before faving faith, or coming to Chrift, is fin ; for *whatfoever is not of faith is fin,* and therefore cannot be a forfaking of fin.

(2.)

(2.) As the above act of Assembly is contrary to the Scripture, order and connection of *duties*, so likewise it is contrary to that order of *gracious operation* held forth in Scripture : For, our *for-saking of sin* (being a branch of true repentance, importing purifi-cation of heart, and the exercise of love, which is the fulfilling of the law) is in Scripture expresly declared to be a fruit of faith, which faith is the soul's *coming* to Christ ; and consequently to maintain, that we must forsake sin in order to our coming to Christ, is as much as to say, we must have repentance, purity of heart and love, in order to our believing in Christ : Whereas, on the contrary, the Lord hath declared in his word, that *faith worketh by love ;* that he *purifies the hearts* of his people *by faith ;* and has promised, that *they shall look* upon him whom they have pierced, and *shall mourn for him.* According to the Assembly's doctrine, our forsaking of sin, which is the removal of the soul's disease, must be at least *com-menced* or *begun*, in order to our coming to him who is the Phy-sician ; and that we must repent of our sin, in order to our coming to him who is exalted to *give repentance* as well as forgiveness of sins : Whereas the Spirit of God, in Scripture, has declared, that *God having raised up his Son Jesus* hath *sent him to bless* us *in turn-ing away every one of us from his iniquities ;* and that sinners are called and invited to *look* and *come* to Christ for salvation both from sin and wrath, and this without regard unto any previous qualifi-cations in them. This *coming* is indeed inconsistent with a resolu-tion to go on in sin ; yet it is plain, that no sinner can wash him-self before he come to the fountain opened for sin and uncleanness : Whereas the Assembly have inverted this order, and have said, up-on the matter, that we must be holy, or so and so qualified, in or-der to our coming to Christ, or having a vital union with him ; which is the very soul of *Neonomian* and *Arminian* doctrine. Ac-cording to Scripture, all gracious actings of the soul, (whereof the *forsaking of sin* is an eminent one) flow from that virtue and influ-ence, which is derived from Christ the true Vine, and that in a way of faith's union with him ; since, without him, or separate from him, we *can do nothing:* And therefore it is vain to pretend to any gracious, evangelical or acceptable act, but by virtue of grace and strength derived from Christ, or until the soul come to Christ, and be united to him, as the living Root, and Fountain of all gracious influence.

(3.) As *forsaking of sin is* no small part of conversion, so the above act of Assembly evidently tends to exalt man's natural powers, and his own ability to convert himself, or prepare himself thereunto ; and thus it greatly favours the *Pelagian* doctrine on this head, expresly contrary to Scripture, which declares, that naturally we are *dead in trespasses and sins ; without strength*, yea, that our *mind is enmity against God.*

Wherefore the Presbytery did, and hereby do, upon the grounds and reasons above mentioned, CONDEMN the following proposi-tions, as *unsound* doctrine. (1.) That (notwithstanding the foresaid gospelgolpel-order and connection of duties) mankind finners muft *forfake* their fins, *in order* to their coming to Chrift, and being inftated in covenant with God. (2.) That a natural man *can* of himfelf forfake his fin ; or, that he can receive any ftrength from Chrift, to *enable* him to forfake fin in a fpiritual and evangelical manner, until, by the power of the Spirit of Chrift working faith in him, he come to Chrift, is united to him, and thus created in Chrift Jefus unto good works. (3.) That any good or commendable qualifications are *required* or *expected* of finners, in the gofpel-call or offer, *in order* to their coming to Chrift, and being inftated in covenant with God. All which propofitions are contrary to the Doctrine held forth from the holy Scriptures in our *Confeffion of Faith*, chap. ix. § 3. " Man " by his fall into a ftate of fin, hath wholly loft all ability of will " to any fpiritual good accompanying falvation ; fo as a natural " man, being altogether averfe from that good, and dead in fin, is " not able, by his own ftrength, to *convert* himfelf, or to *prepare* " himfelf thereunto." And chap. xiv. § 2. where the principal acts of faving faith are faid to be, " accepting, receiving, and refting " upon Chrift alone for——Sanctification," whereof forfaking fin is a branch.

And the Prefbytery *acknowledge, affert* and *declare*, That it is the duty of all, upon the revelation of Chrift in the gofpel, and without looking for any previous qualifications in themfelves, *inftantly* to believe in him for falvation, both from fin and wrath ; and that, in fo doing only, they will be made, in a gofpel manner, to mourn for fin, *forfake it*, and live unto righteoufnefs : So that it is not *poffible* for any man, of himfelf, to forfake his fins, nor is it *confiftent* with the Divine method of grace held forth in the gofpel, that a finner fhould receive ftrength and grace to forfake his fins, or actually to exercife gofpel-repentance, *until* he is determined and enabled by the power of the fpirit of faith, to look or *come* to Chrift, the Prince and Saviour exalted to give repentance and forgivenefs of fins.

Therefore, upon the grounds and reafons forefaid, the Prefbytery *exhort* and *warn* all under their infpection, to be aware of every doctrine that has a tendency to pervert the gofpel-order in the manner above condemned ; or to exalt corrupt nature unto an ability of will to any fpiritual good accompanying falvation : As the above doctrine, of forfaking our fin *in order* to our coming to Chrift, manifeftly doth ; in regard a natural man can no more forfake his fin, or qualify himfelf for the grace of God, than the *Ethiopian* can change his fkin, or the leopard his fpots, according to the doctrine contained in the forefaid paffages of our *Confeffion*, and in our *Larger Catechifm*, 2. 32.

SECTION II. [Concerning the Injuries done to the Doctrine of Grace, by the Affemblies 1720 and 1722.]

OPPOSITION to gofpel-truth did farther appear, when, in the year 1720, the Affembly took occafion from the reprinting of a book entituled

entituled, *The Marrow of Modern Divinity*, with a *preface* by a worthy minifter of this Church, now deceafed, to give a more deep wound to the gofpel-doctrine of *free Grace;* by condemning feveral precious and important truths, through the fides of that book, in the 5th *Act* of the faid Affembly. And although, upon a *reprefentation* given in by fome minifters to the Affembly 1721, laying open the dangerous confequences of the faid *act*, the Affembly that met *anno* 1722, afferted the truth, concerning fome points of doctrine, in the exprefs words of our Confeffion and Catechifms, yet the faid act of Affembly 1720, not only ftands *unrepealed*, but its authority, as a ftanding act in full force, is *maintained* and *confirmed* by Act 7th Affembly 1722, entituled, *Act concerning Doctrine, confirming and explaining the acts 5th and 8th of the General Affembly* anno 1720. In the faid act, ' The General Affembly finds, that the ' faid Affembly 1720, in thefe Acts, had no defign to recede from ' the received doctrine of this Church, nor by them have done in- ' jury to truth, nor given countenance to error———and confi- ' dering, that the *brethren's* defire, that the act 1720 fhould be ' repealed, is unjuft, the Affembly does refufe the fame.' And in regard the faid act 1722 is exprefsly faid to be in *vindication of the* above *two Acts of Affembly* 1720, *and for wiping off* (what they call) *injurious afperfions, caft upon them by the brethren, in their reprefentation;* it plainly follows, that whatever truths may feem to be afferted by the Affembly 1722, they can be underftood in no *other fenfe*, than will agree with the acts of Affembly 1720.

Wherefore although this Prefbytery are far from putting that book entituled the *Marrow of Modern Divinity*, or any other private compofure, upon a level with our approven *ftandards* of Doctrine; or to vindicate every expreffion in that book, or any other private writing, as abfolutely faultlefs : Yet, in regard the Affembly have fingled out the faid book, of all others that have been publifhed, and paffed fuch a peculiar fentence againft it, *ftrictly prohibiting and difcharging all the minifters of this Church to recommend the faid book, and requiring them to warn their people not to read or ufe the fame;* though the difference between the Law and the Gofpel, and between the Covenant of Works and the Covenant of Grace, as alfo the true way of attaining gofpel-holinefs, be therein fet forth in a very clear light. And likewife, in regard that many of the lefs judicious may be impofed upon, to believe that all and every one of the pofitions, condemned in the forefaid *Acts* of Affembly, are *damnable herefies;* when the Affembly 1722 ' do ftrictly prohibit ' and difcharge all the minifters of this Church to ufe, by writing, ' printing, preaching, catechifing, or otherwife teaching, either pub- ' licly or privately, thefe or any of thefe pofitions above menti- ' oned (in their act) or what may be equivalent to them, or of ' like tendency, under the pain of the cenfures of this Church, ' conform to the merit of their offence :' And farther, confidering that, under the colour of condemning the faid book, feveral impor- tant and previous truths are deeply wounded, and the purity of
doctrine-

doctrine contained in our Confeſſion of Faith and Catechiſms, ob-ſcured and perverted : THEREFORE, upon the above and other weighty reaſons, this Preſbytery judge it their duty, to endeavour the preſervation of the purity of doctrine, and that the ſame may be faithfully tranſmitted to ſucceeding generations, by *vindicating* the profeſſed principles of this Church from the injuries done them, in the above-mentioned acts, and *aſſerting* the truth from the holy Scriptures and our ſtandards of Doctrine, in oppoſition to the errors and miſtakes contained in the ſaid acts.

ARTICLE I.   [Of the Injury done to the Doctrine of Grace, under the Head of *Univerſal Atonement and Pardon.*]

THE *firſt* head of Doctrine, as claſſed by the Aſſembly 1720, in their *fifth* act, concerning a book entituled the *Marrow of Modern Divinity*, is concerning the *nature of faith* *. But, becauſe of the relation that there is between faith and the gift or grant that God has made of Chriſt unto mankind in the goſpel-promiſe, and the dependency that faith has thereupon, it will be neceſſary, in order to the more diſtinct opening up of the nature of faith, to take notice firſt of the injuries done to Truth by the foreſaid Aſſembly 1720, act 5. under the head of *Univerſal Atonement* and *Pardon.*

Under this head, the following paſſages are quoted by the Aſſembly, *Marrow*, &c. p. 108. ‘ Chriſt hath taken upon him the ‘ ſins of all men.’ The author's words are, ‘ Chriſt, as man's ſure-‘ ty,———according to that eternal and mutual agreement, that ‘ was betwixt God the Father and him,——put himſelf in the ‘ room and place of all the *faithful*, Iſa. liii. 6. *And the Lord hath* ‘ *laid on him the iniquity of us all.* Then came the law, as it is the ‘ covenant of works, and ſaid (*N. B.* Here the author cites *Lu-* ‘ *ther's* words) I find him a ſinner, yea, ſuch an one as has taken ‘ upon him the ſins of all men, therefore let him die———and ſo ‘ the law———ſet upon him, and killed him ; and by this means ‘ was the juſtice of God fully ſatisfied, his wrath appeaſed, and all ‘ true believers acquitted from all their ſins,’ &c.

The next paſſage quoted by the Aſſembly is p. 119. ‘ The Fa-‘ ther hath made a deed of gift and grant unto all mankind, that ‘ whoſoever of them all ſhall believe in his Son, ſhall not periſh, ‘ &c. i. e. (whoſoever believes or is perſuaded that Chriſt is his, ‘ for this muſt be the ſenſe, according to the former paſſages.) ‘ Hence it was that Chriſt ſaid to his diſciples, *Go and preach the* ‘ *goſpel to every creature under heaven;* that is, go and tell every ‘ man without exception, that here is good news for him, *Chriſt is* ‘ *dead for him.*’ The author adds, *and if he will take him and ac-cept of his righteouſneſs, he ſhall have him.* Here the author brings
in

---

* The Aſſembly condemned the doctrine of that book, under ſix general heads, viz 1. Concerning the nature of faith. 2. Of univerſal atonement and pardon. 3. Holineſs not neceſſary to ſalvation. 4. Fear of puniſhment and hope of reward,—not allowed to be motives of a believer's obedience. 5. That the believer is not under the law, as a rule of life. 6. The ſix Antinomian paradoxes.

in the fimilitude of a good king, caufing a proclamation to be made
through his whole kingdom, that all rebels and banifhed men fhall
fafely return home, becaufe, at the fuit and defert of fome dear
friend of theirs, it hath pleafed the king to pardon them. ' Cer-
' tainly (fays the author) none of thefe *rebels* ought to doubt, but
' he *fhall obtain* true pardon for this *rebellion*, and fo return home,
' and live under the fhadow of that gracious *king.*' Then follows
the quotation of the Affembly, ' even fo our good *King*, the Lord
' of Heaven and earth, hath for the obedience and defert of our
' good brother Jefus Chrift, pardoned all our fins.' It is added by
the author, ' and made a proclamation throughout the whole world,
' that every one of us may fafely return to God, in Jefus Chrift.
' Wherefore (fays he) I befeech you make no doubt of it, but *draw*
' *near with a true heart in full affurance of faith*, Heb. x. 22.' The
Affembly likewife quote p. 127, 128, where the author is exhort-
ing and encouraging finners, to come to Chrift or believe in him,
notwithftanding of their fins and the aggravations of them, from
the Scriptures, *This is a faithful faying and worthy of all acceptation,
that Chrift Jefus came into the world to fave finners ; the whole need
not a phyfician, but they that are fick ; he came not to call the righteous, but finners to repentance.* The Affembly's judgment upon the
above paffages, is as follows. ' Here is afferted an univerfal re-
' demption as to purchafe, contrary to *John* x. 10. 15, 27, 28, 29.
' and xv. 13. and xvii. *Titus* ii. 14. *Conf.* chap. iii. § 6. chap. viii.
' §. 8. *Larger Cat.* Q. 59.'

There is nothing in the above paffages, that in the leaft counte-
nances *univerfal redemption as to purchafe*, a doctrine which the
Prefbytery rejects and condemns, as contrary to the Scriptures, and
places of our Confeffion and Catechifms quoted by the Affembly.
Nor can the author of the *Marrow* be juftly cenfured for venting
any fuch error; for he plainly teacheth, through the whole of his book,
that Chrift reprefented, and fuffered for *none but the elect*, as p. 108.
' Chrift put himfelf in the room and place of all the faithful ;' by
which he underftands the elect, as he exprefsly declares in the firft
fentence of his preface, ' Jefus Chrift, the fecond *Adam*, did, as a
' common perfon, enter into covenant with God his Father, for all
' the elect, that is to fay fays he) all thofe that have or fhall be-
' lieve on his name,' whereas the *Univerfalifts* contend, that God,
in fending of Chrift, had no refpect to *fome*, more than to *others*,
but deftined Chrift for a Saviour to *all* men alike.

As the author has exprefsly declared himfelf for a *particular* redemption and reprefentation ; fo neither will the above paffages,
quoted by the Affembly, bear the charge of an univerfal redemption as to *purchafe*. The firft paffage from the *Marrow*, p. 108,
' Chrift hath taken upon him the fins of all men,' is part of a fentence quoted from *Luther* on the *Galatians*, and is fufficiently guard-
ed againft the charge of univerfal redemption as to purchafe, by
what the author fays immediately before and after the faid paffage, as above. As to the next condemned pofition, *God the Fa-*

ther

ther hath made a deed of *Gift* and *Grant* unto *all mankind, that who-soever of them all shall believe in his Son, shall not perish but have everlasting life,* will indeed bear a sufficiency of worth and *merit* in the Sacrifice of Christ, for the salvation of all men, and the removal of all legal bars that stood in the sinner's way ; and that Christ crucified, is the ordinance of God for the salvation of mankind, in the use-making of which only they can be saved ; and consequently a full warrant to gospel-ministers, to proclaim these glad tidings unto every man, and a warrant to all and every one to believe these glad tidings, with particular application to their own souls : But all this will not infer an *universal* atonement or redemption as to *purchase.* Neither will the following words infer any such charge, ' Go and preach the gospel to every creature under heaven, that ' is, go and tell every man without exception, that here is good ' news for him, Christ is dead for him, and if he will take him, ' and accept of his righteousness, he shall have him.' It is manifest from the book itself, that the author's design in quoting the above passage from Dr *Preston's* Treatise of faith, is not to determine concerning the *extent of Christ's death,* but to discover the warrant that sinners have to believe in Christ, namely, the *unlimited offer and free gift* of Christ to every man in the world, which necessarily supposes, that Christ crucified is the ordinance of God for salvation to mankind, as distinguished from fallen angels ; and therefore the obvious meaning of the expression must be, tell every man that Christ is dead for him, i. e. *for him to come to,* or *believe on,* for salvation : even as it might be said to the manslayer of old, that the city of refuge was prepared and open *for him to fly to,* that he might be safe : And this is what the author of the *Marrow,* according to Scripture, declares, that every man ought to be persuaded of, namely, that Christ is the ordinance and gift of God, for salvation to *him* in particular ; which is quite contrary to the doctrine of the *Arminians,* who deny a *particular* persuasion to be in faith, upon the free offer in the gospel, as to the person's own salvation.

Since then it appears, from the sense and meaning of the author, that the above passages cannot be interpreted, as favouring universal redemption as to *purchase,* there must be something else intended by the condemnatory sentence of the Assembly. And it will be obvious, from the tenor and strain of the Assembly's *Act,* that, under the misapplied title of universal redemption as to *purchase,* they condemn the universal and unlimited *offer* of Christ unto mankind sinners *as such.* For, although the Assembly 1722 seems to own, that the Revelation of the Divine will in the word affords a warrant to offer Christ unto all, and a warrant to all to receive him ; yet they can own that *warrant,* only in a consistency with their notion of *faith,* that is, a warrant only for the *elect,* or those who are *so and so qualified* to receive Christ ; but they do not own, that mankind sinners, *as such,* however sinful and miserable, have any such warrant : And consequently, the Revelation of the Divine will in the word, making such a gift of Christ to the world of
mankind

mankind finners *as such,*—as affords a warrant to offer Chrift unto all without exception, or to preach the gofpel to *every creature,* and a warrant to all to receive him : and the fovereign grace that has made this grant, or deed of gift, not to devils, but to men ; are encroached upon and injured by the Acts of both Affemblies, *Annis* 1720 and 1722.

The Scripture exprefsly afferteth, *John* iii. 27. *A man can receive nothing except it be given him from above ;* and therefore the receiving of Chrift neceffarily prefuppofeth a *giving* of him. There may be indeed a *giving* of Chrift where there is no *receiving,* as this is the great fin of the generality of the hearers of the gofpel, who will not come unto him that they may have life : But, in no cafe, could there be a *receiving* of Chrift for falvation, if there were not a *giving* of him before ; or, which is the fame thing, a revelation of him in the word, affording a warrant for finners, *as such,* to receive him. Now, this deed of gift, or grant made to all mankind in the word, is the very foundation of our faith, and the ground and warrant of the *ministerial offer,* without which no minifter could have authority to preach the gofpel to every creature, or to make a full, free and unhampered offer of Chrift, his grace, righteoufnefs and falvation, to all mankind to whom they have accefs in providence.

This deed of gift, or grant of Chrift in the word, unto mankind finners as fuch, is exprefsly fet forth in feveral texts of Scripture. *Isa.* ix. 6. *Unto us a Child is born, unto us a Son is given.* John iii. 16. *God so loved the world, that he gave his only begotten Son ; that whosoever believeth in him should not perish, but have everlasting life.* Chap. vi. 32. *My Father giveth you the true bread from Heaven.* Acts iv. 12.—*For there is none other name under Heaven given among men whereby we must be saved.* 1 John v. 11. *This is the record that God hath given to us eternal life, and this life is in his Son.* Rev. xxii. 17.—*Whosoever will, let him take of the water of life freely.* From which Scriptures the following truths are evidently clear.

(1.) Although the purchafe and application of redemption be peculiar to the *elect,* yet the warrant to receive Chrift is common to *all,* as they are finful men and women of *Adam's* family, Prov. viii. 5. *Unto you, O men, I call, and my voice is to the sons of men.*

(2.) The *giving* mentioned in the above texts is not to be underftood of a giving into *possession,* which is peculiar to them only who believe ; but it is a giving by way of *offer,* whereupon one *may* take poffeffion ; or fuch a giving as warrants a man to believe, or receive the gift, and therefore muft be *anterior* to actual believing ; even as the manna behoved to be given, or rained down, *before* it could be tafted or fed upon : And thus *God gave his only begotten Son, that whosoever believeth on him should not perish, but have everlasting life ;* From whence it follows, that Chrift is the Saviour of the world, and his falvation a *common salvation, Jude ver.* 3. So that mankind loft have a *common* intereft in him, which fallen angels have

not ;

not; it being lawful and warrantable for us, not for them, to take possession of Christ, and the whole of his salvation.

(3.) The persons to whom this grant and offer is made, are not the *elect only*, but mankind considered *as lost*. For the *Record* of God, being such a thing as *warrants* all to believe on the Son of God, as appears from the above Scriptures, it is evident, that it can be no such warrant, to tell men that God hath given eternal life to the *elect*; as the offering of a gift to a certain *select* company, can never be a warrant for *all* men to receive or take possession of it.

This will further appear if it is considered, that the great sin of unbelief lies, in not believing the *record, that God hath given us e-ternal life.* Unbelief doth not consist in a mere disbelieving of that proposition, that God hath given eternal life to the *elect*; for the most despairing unbeliever may be persuaded hereof, and their belief of it adds to their anguish and torment: But they do not set to their seal that God *is true;* on the contrary, they make God a liar, in not believing the record of God, even that he hath *given unto them* eternal life in his Son Jesus Christ; as hereby they deny the *faithfulness* of God in that record, and his being indeed in earnest in that grant and gift of Christ, made unto sinners, *as such*, in the gospel: They slight and despise the *authority* of a God of grace, commanding them to give this answer of a particular applying faith, unto the offer of his grace in his word, and his call to receive the same; and so flying in the face of God's Record and Testimony, who deservedly perish in *unbelief*, seeing the kingdom and gift of God was brought *near* to them in the offer of the gospel, and they would not take it.

The above doctrine concerning the *gift* of Christ in the word, unto mankind sinners, is likewise from the holy Scriptures asserted in our Confession of Faith and Catechisms, particularly, *Con.* Chap. vii. § 3. ' He freely offereth unto sinners, life and salvation by Jesus ' Christ; requiring of them faith in him, that they may be saved, ' and promising his Holy Spirit, to make them willing and able to ' believe.' Where it is plain, that the offer of life and salvation, is unto mankind, considered *as sinners;* and that, therefore, sinners, *as such*, have a warrant to believe, or receive the unspeakable gift of God, according to the Scriptures quoted in the *Confession*, Mark xvi. 15, 16.—*Go ye unto all the world, and preach the gospel to every creature. He that believeth and is baptized, shall be saved; but he that believeth not, shall be damned.* John iii. 16. *God so loved the world*, &c. And the same doctrine is also taught, *Larger Cat.* Quest. 63.

Wherefore the Presbytery *did*, and *hereby do*, for the grounds and reasons above mentioned, *acknowledge, declare* and *assert*, that God the Father moved by nothing, but his free love to mankind lost, hath made a deed of *gift and grant*, of his Son Jesus Christ, unto mankind, in the word, that whosoever of them all shall receive this gift by a true and lively faith, shall not perish, but have everlasting life: Or, which is the same thing, that there is a revelation of the

the Divine will in the word, affording a warrant to offer Christ unto *all* mankind without exception, and a warrant to *all* freely to receive him, however great sinners they are, or have been ; and that this gift is made to *mankind* only, and not to fallen angels ; according to the doctrine held forth from the Scriptures and our Confession above-quoted.

And the Presbytery hereby *reject* and *condemn* the following tenets and opinions, contained in or couched under the forefaid acts of Assembly. (1.) That the free, unlimited and universal *offer* of Christ in the gospel, to sinners of mankind, as such, is inconsistent with particular *redemption;* or, that God the Father his making a *deed of gift* unto all mankind, that whosoever of them all shall believe on his Son, shall not perish, but have everlasting life, infers an *universal atonement*, or redemption as to purchase. (2.) That this grant or offer is made only to the *elect*, or to such who have *previous* qualifications commending them above others. Which doctrines are quite contrary to the passages of Scripture, and our Confession of Faith above-quoted.

ARTICLE II. [Of the Injury done to the Doctrine of Grace,] *concerning the Nature of Faith.*

The Assembly 1722 do only take notice of the *definition* of faith in the *Marrow*, without mentioning the other passages quoted by the Assembly 1720, and by them condemned under that head : Which might seem to give ground to apprehend that the Assembly 1722 had passed from any *vindication* of what the Assembly 1720 had done in condemning these and other passages and quotations, as contrary to the holy Scriptures, our Confession of Faith and Catechisms; especially when they say, ' That the said passages are condemned *only in so far as* they import the said erroneous opinions,' ascribed unto them. Yet, as *truth* was never, in any age, condemned under the notion of *truth*, but of *error :* And, whereas the title of the act of Assembly 1722 shews that it is designed for *confirming* as well as explaining the Act 1720 ; and that not only is there no honour done to condemned truth, by an acknowledgment of an error in the management of the said Assembly 1720 ; but their act continues to stand in full force among those designed for public use : Upon these and the like grounds, the Presbytery *find* that the truth contained in these passages, is not only left bleeding, but has received a further *wound* by the said Assembly 1722. Wherefore, though the Presbytery do not find it expedient to insist on every particular expression or proposition, condemned by that Assembly 1720 : Yet they judge it necessary, for the vindication of truth, and as a mean of transmitting it in its purity unto after ages, to take notice of some of the propositions condemned by the said Assembly ; particularly, page 118. ' There is *no more* for him (*viz.* man) to do, but only to know and believe, that Christ hath done *all for him*.' The passage relative to
this

this fubject in the faid page ftands thus, ' All the covenant that be-
' lievers are to have regard unto for life and falvation, is the
' free and gracious covenant that is betwixt Chrift, or God in
' Chrift, and them.   And; in this covenant, there is not any *con-*
' *dition* or *law* to be performed on man's part, by himfelf : No ;
' there is no more for him to do, but only to know and believe
' that Chrift hath done *all for him.*——Here you are to *work no-*
' *thing*, here you are to *do nothing*, here you are to *render nothing*
' unto God ; but only to *receive* the treafure, which is Jefus Chrift,
' and apprehend him in your heart by faith ;——fo fhall you ob-
' tain forgivenefs of fins, righteoufnefs and eternal happinefs,——
' not by *doing*, but by *receiving.*   Nothing here cometh *betwixt*,
' but faith, only apprehending Chrift in the promife.'   Then the
following words, p. 119. which immediately follow what is above,
are particularly cited as erroneous : ' This then is perfect righteouf-
' nefs (thefe words are here omitted by them, *to hear nothing, to*
' *know nothing, to do nothing of the law of works, but*) only to
' know and believe, that Jefus Chrift is now gone to the Father,
' and fitteth at his right hand, not as a judge, but *as made unto you*
' *of God, Wifdom, Righteoufnefs, Sanctification and Redemption.*'
    The next paffage condemned by the Affembly, is quoted by the
Author from Dr *Prefton* on Faith, *Marrow*, p. 120.   ' For as
' much as the holy Scriptures fpeaketh to *all* in general, *none* of us
' ought to diftruft himfelf, but believe that it doth belong *parti-*
' *cularly* to himfelf.'   They alfo refer to feveral other pages of the
Marrow, without condefcending upon the expreffions that relate to
the nature of faith.   But the doctrine contained in the above paffages, and likewife in the paffages referred to by the Affembly,
in *fo far* as they refpect the nature of faith, will be illuftrated by
what fhall be faid in vindication of the Author's account of juftifying faith, as quoted by the Affembly from p. 119.——' Where-
' fore as *Paul* and *Silas* faid to the jailor, fo fay I unto you, *Be-*
' *lieve on the Lord Jefus Chrift and thou fhalt be faved*, that is, be
' verily perfuaded in your heart, that Jefus Chrift is *yours*, and that
' *you* fhall have life and falvation by him ; that whatfoever Chrift
' did for the redemption of mankind, he did it for *you.*'   The
judgment of the Affembly 1720 upon this head, is as follows,
' This Notion of *faving faith* appears contrary to Scripture, *Ifa.* 1.
' 10. *Rom.* viii. 16. 1 *John* v. 13. and to *Confeff.* Chap. xviii. § 1,
' 3, 4. and to *Larger Catechifm*, Queft. 81. 172. all which paffages
' fhew, that affurance is not of the effence of faith ; whereas the paf-
' fages cited from the *Marrow, &c.* appear to affert the contrary,
' making that *faving faith*, commanded in the gofpel, a man's per-
' fuafion that Chrift *is his*, and died *for him*, and that whoever hath
' not this perfuafion or affurance, hath not anfwered the gofpel-
' call, nor is a true believer.'
    The general Affembly *Anno* 1722, in their 7th act confirming
and explaining the above act of Affembly 1720, vindicate the faid
act upon this head, and particularly condemn the Author of the
                                                          Marrow

Marrow for making that to be the juftifying act of faving faith;
' A man's being perfuaded that Chrift *is his*, and that *he* fhall have
' life and falvation by him, and that whatfoever Chrift did for the
' redemption of mankind, he did it *for him.*' And all the account
which that Affembly give of faith is as follows, ' That a belief
' and perfuafion of the mercy of God in Chrift, and of Chrift's abi-
' lity and willingnefs to fave *all that come* unto him, is neceffary
' unto juftifying faith.'

The Prefbytery judge it their duty to enquire fomewhat particularly into the nature of *faith*, above defcribed : in regard that a
right notion of the nature of faith, as revealed in the holy Scriptures, and agreeably thereto, fet down in our ftandards of doctrine,
is fo *neceffary* to the falvation of a finner, and that the fame has
been fo much *darkened* by the Affemblies of this Church. For although the Affembly 1722 feems to refufe the charge of excluding
from the nature of faith its *appropriating act*, yet it is impoffible to
vindicate them from it ; in regard they fpeak of no other affurance
in faith, but a *perfuafion of the mercy of God in Chrift, and of
Chrift's ability and willingnefs to fave all that come unto him*, which
is a perfuafion that *devils* and *reprobates* may have. And, in agree-
ablenefs to this view of faith, they condemn the affurance which
the Author of the *Marrow* advanceth, when he makes that to be
the juftifying act of faith, ' A man's being perfuaded that Chrift
' *is his;* that *he* fhall have life and falvation by him, and that
' whatfoever Chrift did for the redemption of mankind, he did it
' *for him.*——Which (fay the Affembly) is contrary to the *texts*
' *of Scripture, and paffages of our Confeffion and Larger Catechifm*
' cited by the Affembly 1720.'

But it will be obvious to any who confiders thefe places of *Scripture*, and paffages of our *Confeffion* and *Larger Catechifm*, quoted by
the Affembly, that they fpeak directly of the *affurance of fenfe*, or
reflection ; whereby believers are certainly affured, that they are
in a ftate of grace, upon the evidence of thefe *marks*, which the
Lord has given of his own work in the foul ; and not of the *affurance* which is in *faith*, in the *direct act* thereof, and which is founded upon the *word* allenarly. For the queftion here is not concerning the *prefent ftate* of the *perfon*, which he is called to examine,
according to the rules of God's Word : The *believer* being called
to examine himfelf, whether he be in the faith, that in the ufe of
appointed means, he may grow up to the full affurance of his being in a ftate of grace, which fhall iffue in complete and eternal
falvation; and the *unbeliever*, or natural man, being called to examine himfelf, that he may be fo far from believing that he is in
a gracious ftate, that he may be perfuaded of the quite contrary, or
that he is at prefent in a ftate of condemnation and wrath, fo as he
may be convinced of the neceffity of believing on the Son of God,
who is come to feek and to fave that which was loft. But the queftion is concerning the *nature* of that *faith*, which all the hearers of
the gofpel are called unto, and which the Scripture plainly defcribes

t

to be a *believing* in God, and a *trusting* in his salvation, a *receiving* of Christ, a *believing* the record, that God hath given *unto us* eternal life, that he will be *our* God, and that *we* shall be his people; and so calling him *our* Father, *our* Husband, *our* God, upon the warrant of his own word of grace. Believers indeed may be frequently in the dark as to the *reality* of their faith, and their present saving possession of eternal life; and there is nothing in the *Marrow* denying or opposing this, yea, on the contrary, it is plainly asserted: But there is a great difference between the *assurance of our state of grace*, which respects the state we are in already, and the *assurance of the promise* of salvation; or, an assured faith of righteousness and salvation in Christ Jesus, as held forth to every sinner of *Adam's* race, to whom the gospel comes, to be received and applied by them, for their *own benefit*; according to that awful caution, *Heb.* iv. 1. *Let us therefore fear, least a promise being left us, of entering into his rest, any of you should seem to come short of it,* viz. by unbelief, as is clear from the context. For, by this assurance or persuasion of Faith, and confidence in a promising God in Christ, we take possession of salvation, as presented to us in the *promise,* and thus we enter into *rest,* Heb. iv. 11. But that assurance spoken of in the articles of our *Confession* of Faith and *Catechism,* cited by the Assembly, is an assurance that the faith which *we have,* is indeed the faith of God's *elect;* or, that we are in a gracious *state,* the issue whereof shall be in full and complete salvation; which assurance is founded upon the evidence of the *reality* of our faith, by comparing it with the marks thereof in Scripture, the connection stated in Scripture between these evidences and salvation, and the testimony of the Spirit, shining on his own work in the soul, and witnessing with our spirits, that *we* are the children of God. From all which it follows, that the passages of Scripture and our standards, quoted by the Assembly, do by no means condemn the assurance which is in the *direct act* of faith, or the *appropriating* persuasion of faith, corresponding to the gift of Christ in the gospel to every sinner in particular. And since the above Act of Assembly plainly doth this, when it is therein expressly denied to belong to the justifying act of faith, ‘ A man's being *persuaded* that Jesus Christ *is his;* ‘ and that *he* shall have life and salvation by him ; and that what- ‘ soever Christ did for the redemption of mankind he did it *for* ‘ *him.*’ It is therefore necessary to vindicate this account of justifying faith, *as agreeable to the holy Scriptures,* and our *standards of doctrine ;* while the excluding of an *appropriating* persuasion from the nature of faith, tends effectually to *shut* that door of access unto the Lord Jesus, which God has *opened,* by the grant that he has made of Christ in the gospel to sinners of mankind, in exclusion of the angels that fell.

I. That the general nature of *faith,* as it is opposite to *unbelief* or doubting, consists in a persuasion of the reality of what is testified, is what cannot be well refused ; and it can as little be reasonably denied, that, where the Testimony to be believed is a *promise* of

good

good to be communicated, a man's faith of that Teſtimony neceſſarily includes his believing the certain accompliſhment of that promiſe to *him*, and his confidence in the perſon who has given the promiſe, that he *will do as he has ſaid.* And it is no leſs evident, that when an *offer* is made in a word of grace, to be received by faith, a perſon does not by faith receive that which is offered, unleſs he believe it is *his*, by virtue, or upon the warrant of that offer made of it to him. And ſo, if a King ſhall make a proclamation of a pardon and indemnity to rebels, and his ſervants, by warrant from him, ſhall ſay to all the rebels in his kingdom, To *you* is this proclamation of grace ſent; a man muſt ſurely either believe the pardon of *his own* crime of rebellion in particular, or elſe *reject* the King's proclamation of grace. Neither will it avail that the man believes *in general*, that there is a pardon proclaimed to rebels *in general:* This they may believe who *need* it not, as being loyal ſubjects; and this they may alſo believe who *reject* it, and continue in their rebellion. Yet the *particular* perſuaſion above-mentioned, is that which the Aſſembly here denies to belong to the *nature* of the juſtifying act of faith; and thereby do really turn juſtifying faith into that *Popiſh* general faith *abjured* by our National Covenant; or they make it a faith to be built, in whole or in part, upon ſomething *wrought in*, or *done by* us; whether our act of believing or repenting, or what elſe, needs not here be inſiſted on.

That juſtifying faith has in it an *appropriating* perſuaſion, or a man's being perſuaded that Chriſt is *his* in particular, is further evident from the following reaſons.

(1.) When a man's conſcience is truly awakened, and convinced by the Spirit of God, as a Spirit of conviction, the man then ſees *himſelf* in particular bound under the curſe; the law accuſing and condemning *him* in particular, ſaying, *Thou* haſt ſinned, and therefore *thou* art curſed: For, *curſed is every one that continueth not in all things which are written in the book of the law, to do them,* Gal. iii. 10. And therefore faith, whereby the blood of Jeſus is apprehended and improven for cleanſing the conſcience from guilt, and looſing that bond of the curſe, muſt *appropriate* and apply Chriſt, as made a curſe for the ſinner in particular, to deliver *him* from the curſe of the law; otherways the goſpel-revelation and offer of Chriſt could not be found *ſuitable* to the man's particular caſe; neither would the free gift be found to be as full unto *juſtification,* as the offence through the law was unto *condemnation;* which were contrary to Gal. iii. 13. *Chriſt hath redeemed us from the curſe of the law, being made a curſe for us; for it is written, curſed is every one that hangeth on a tree.* Rom. v. 18—21. *Therefore, as by the offence of one, judgment came upon all men to condemnation; even ſo, by the righteouſneſs of one, the free gift came upon all men to juſtification of life. For, as by one man's diſobedience many were made ſinners; ſo by the obedience of one ſhall many be made righteous. Moreover, the law entered, that the offence might abound; but where ſin abounded, grace did much more abound: That as ſin hath reigned unto*

D   *death,*

death, even so might grace reign through righteousness unto eternal life, by Jesus Christ our Lord. And here it may be observed, that, as a man having only a general faith of the *law*, as condemning sinners in general, will easily rest in a general faith of the *gospel*, or of Christ's willingness and ability to save sinners, or to save them that come to him : So one brought by Divine convincing power to a special faith of the *Law*, as what particularly is directed against *him* for his condemnation, such a person's conscience cannot be satisfied, nor will it absolve him, or he be purged from guilt, till he has got the special faith of the *gospel*, or of the mercy of God in Christ, as reaching to *him* in particular ; or be made to believe in particular for *himself*, that Christ is *his*, and that *he* shall have life and salvation by him.

(2.) A man's being persuaded that Christ is *his*, is necessary to answer the *call* or *offer* of the gospel, according to the deed of gift or grant that God has made of Christ in the Word. Now, salvation is offered to *every one* in particular, that hears these glad tidings, *Acts* ii. 39. *The promise is unto you ;* and therefore it is certain, that faith, which is the answer of the soul to the call of God in the gospel, must lay hold on salvation for the person in *particular.* For, suppose that the offer of the gospel be to *all* in general ; yet, if a man is not influenced by the holy Spirit, to *appropriate* to himself the *common salvation*, or what did lie before in common, in the gospel-offer, he cannot be said to receive or close with Christ *as* offered therein. Wherefore the Assembly, by denying this appropriating persuasion to be in the nature of faith, fly in the face of the Scriptures of truth, *Acts* iii. 26. *Unto you first, God having raised up his Son Jesus, sent him to bless you, in turning away every one of you from his iniquities.* Isa. xlv. 22. *Look unto me, and be ye saved, all the ends of the earth.* Which Scriptures, and many others that might be quoted to this purpose, plainly require an *appropriating* act of faith from every one, without which there can be no answering the Testimony of God therein revealed. Doth the Testimony of God run out in such terms, *Unto you is the word of this salvation sent ; the promise is unto you ; whosoever will, let him take ?* Then the act of faith, corresponding to such a Testimony, must certainly be an appropriating persuasion, *Surely shall one say, in the Lord have I righteousness.* And this no way contradicts what is frequently found, in the sad experience of the believer, who may want the comfort of his faith for a long time, and have sad mixtures of darkness and unbelief attending its exercise, so as to doubt of the reality of his faith, or that it is of a right kind. For still *doubting* can no more be said to be in the nature of *faith*, because it frequently takes place in the believer, by reason of prevailing unbelief and indwelling sin, than darkness can be said to be in the nature of the Sun, because he is sometimes eclipsed : for faith and doubting are in their own nature *opposite :* And therefore, though a true believer is not at all times assured of his being presently in a state of grace, and capable thence to draw the conclusion, that he

shall

ſhall be ſaved; but may wait long before he obtain this aſſurance, according to our Confeſſion and Catechiſms; yet this ſays nothing againſt that man's being perſuaded that Chriſt is *his*, according as Chriſt is held out and made over in the promiſe unto *him*. And further, if the Aſſembly, by condemning the appropriating perſuaſion of faith, thereby meant to limit and reſtrict the object of the *external offer* of Chriſt unto the *elect* only, then this alſo is plainly contrary to Scripture, *Prov.* viii. 4. ' Unto you, O men, I call; and " my voice is unto the ſons of men. *Acts* xiii. 47. I have ſet " thee to be a light of the Gentiles, that thou ſhouldſt be for ſalva- " tion unto the ends of the earth. *Mark* xvi. 15. Go ye into all " the world, and preach the goſpel to every creature."

From all this it is evident, that the faith of the operation of God, muſt anſwer and correſpond to the Teſtimony and Record of God, which is the foundation of it: So that, when he ſays unto us as ſinners, *I am the Lord thy God*, it is our duty to ſay, *This God is our God for ever and ever;* or, which is the ſame thing, to be perſuaded that Chriſt is *ours*, and God, our God in him. This is farther evident if it is conſidered,

(3.) What is the Lord's *name* revealed to us. We cannot but *deny* his name without this appropriating perſuaſion, that he is *ours;* for his name is JEHOVAH OUR RIGHTEOUSNESS, *the light of the Gentiles*. Thus he ſpeaks to the whole viſible Church, I AM THE LORD YOUR GOD: Yea, his name is *Salvation to the ends of the earth*. And, as he commands to proclaim his name, and preach this goſpel to every creature; ſo the anſwer of faith, which correſponds to this Teſtimony and record of God as the foundation of it, muſt be, He is Jehovah *my* Righteouſneſs, *my* Light, *my* Salvation. The Lord *my* God: Otherwiſe we refuſe to own him by that name by which he has revealed himſelf to us, and do thus deny his name.

(4.) The *command* of God does farther evince this truth, that it is the indiſpenſible duty of every hearer of the goſpel thus to believe in the Lord Jeſus Chriſt, even to be verily perſuaded that Jeſus Chriſt is *his*. For, in the preface to the ten Commandments, God makes over himſelf to ſinners as *their* God and Redeemer; And, as all the Commandments are directed to every one in particular, ſo the *firſt* Commandment, *Thou ſhalt have no other Gods before me*, requires every one to know and acknowledge the Lord to be *his* God and Redeemer. On this head, we · are taught, *Larger Cat.* queſt. 104. That our *truſting* in God is the ſuitable exerciſe of that acknowledging of him as the only true God and *our* God, which is there required. And this is a clear evidence, that there can be no truſting in God *without* faith's perſuaſion of his being *our* God: Whence, according to the Word of God and our received ſtandards, there can be no *truſting* in Chriſt without faith's perſuaſion that Chriſt is *ours*, the great God our · Saviour, *Iſa.* xii. 2. *Behold God is my ſalvation; I will truſt and not be afraid.*

(5.) The appropriating act of faith is further illuſtrated from the *covenant-relation* betwixt Chriſt and the whole viſible Church, which in
Scrip-

Scripture, is commonly fet forth under the fimilitude of a *marriage-relation* betwixt hufband and wife ; as, *Ifa.* liv. 1. *More are the children of the defolate, than the children of the married wife ;* where the Church of the *Jews* is faid to be *married* to the Lord : And hence, apoftafy from his worfhip, doctrine and laws, to which they are bound by Covenant, is called *adultery* and *whoredom, Ezek.* xvi. *Hof.* 1. and in many other places. Thus we find, when the Lord would reclaim a backfliding Church from her defections and apoftafies, he is pleafed, in a way of fovereign grace, to urge them thereunto from the confideration of this *marriage-relation* betwixt him and them ; as, *Jer.* iii. 1. *Though thou haft played the harlot with many lovers, yet return again unto me :* and verfe 14, *Turn, O backfliding children, faith the Lord, for I am married unto you.* Now, the anfwer of faith which God challenges, is verfe 4. *Wilt thou not, from this time, cry unto me, my Father ; thou art the Guide of my youth ?* And, when he promifes to make his grace fufficient for them to this end, it is in terms of *appropriation,* verfe 19.—*And I faid, Thou fhalt call me, my Father, and fhalt not turn away from me :* And fo, when they actually turn to the Lord, they take up their relation to him by covenant, as the leading motive of their return by faith, faying, as in verfe 22.—*Behold, we come unto thee for thou art the Lord our God.* Indeed, this appropriation of faith juft cor- · refponds unto the promife or grant of grace made to the vifible Church, as the *echo* to the *voice,* Zech. xiii. 9.——*I will fay, it is my people : And they fhall fay, The Lord is my God ;* and in this way, the foul is *betrothed unto* him *for ever, in righteoufnefs, in judgment, in loving-kindnefs and in mercies.*

II. The Affembly moreover deny, that it belongs to the juftifying act of faith, a man's being perfuaded *that he fhall have life and falvation by Chrift :* But there can be no true faith without this perfuafion in fome meafure or degree. For, faith is a believing the promife, *and this is the promife that he hath promifed us, even eternal life :* It is a believing the record, and this is the record, *That God hath given to us eternal life, and this life is in his Son.* Hence, this perfuafion, *That we fhall have life and falvation by Chrift,* is the fame thing with a believing on the Son, or a refting on him for falvation. It is evident that none can believe on Chrift, truft in him or reft on him for falvation, without fome degree of perfuafion, that *they* fhall have life and falvation by him, *viz.* a falvation from fin as well as from wrath : And accordingly, we find the faints of God in Scripture, expreffing themfelves in the terms of this perfuafion ; Acts xv. 11. *We believe that, through the grace of the Lord Jefus Chrift, we fhall be faved ;* Micah vii. 7.——*I will wait for the God of my falvation :* So that without this perfuafion, that *we fhall* have life and falvation by Chrift, we do not fet to our feal that God is *true,* nor give that anfwer of faith, which the Lord points out, as the only fuitable anfwer unto his call of *Looking unto him for falvation.*

III.

III. The third part of the defcription of faith *condemned* by the Affembly is, *That whatfoever Chrift did for the redemption of mankind, he did it for you.* But this branch of the perfuafion of faith the Apoftle affirms, when he fays, *Gal.* ii. 20.—*I live by the faith of the Son of God, who loved me, and gave himfelf for me.* It is certain, that what Chrift *did* for the redemption of mankind, was his obedience unto the death in their room : And this his doing and fuffering is that furety-righteoufnefs, which, as the fecond *Adam*, he has wrought for us, and for the fake of which the Lord is well pleafed. Now this perfect righteoufnefs is brought near to every one of us in the gofpel, even to the *flout-hearted and far from righteoufnefs*, and is laid in *Zion* as the foundation of our acceptance with God, and hope of eternal life and falvation ; fo that this perfuafion, that *whatfoever Chrift did for the redemption of mankind, he did it for us*, muft, in connection with the former, enter into the *nature* of that faith, which anfwers the call and revelation of God in his Word : And accordingly, we find the faith of the operation of God correfponding herewith, expreffed, Ifa. xlv. 24. *Surely, fhall one fay, in the Lord have I righteoufnefs and ftrength.*

Upon the whole, the Affembly, by condemning the above defcription of faith, have both condemned the Scripture-account of the true nature of faith, and alfo the fcriptural *order*, in which faith appropriates or clofes with its object : For the *firft* thing to be believed, or to be perfuaded of, upon the revelation of the grant that God has made of Chrift unto mankind finners in the Word, is, That *Chrift is ours ;* upon which there will *follow*, according to the meafure of faith, a perfuafion, That *we fhall have life and falvation by him*, and that *whatfoever he did for the redemption of mankind, he did it for us.*

This account of the nature of faith, is the fame with what is contained in our approven ftandards of Doctrine before the year 1647. *Palatine* Catechifm (taught in this and other reformed Churches) *Queft.* ' What is true faith ? *Anf.* It is an *affured affi-* ' *ance* kindled in my heart by the Holy Ghoft, by which I reft ' upon God, *making fure account* that forgivenefs of fins, everlaft- ' ing righteoufnefs and life, is *beftowed*, not only upon others, but alfo ' upon ME, and that freely by the mercy of God, for the merit ' and defert of Chrift alone.' *Old* Conf. Art. iii. ' Regeneration ' is wrought by the power of the Holy Ghoft, working in the hearts ' of the elect of God, an *affured* faith in the Promife of God, ' revealed *to us* in his Word, by which faith we apprehend Chrift ' Jefus, with the graces and benefits promifed in him.' Unto which agrees the Catechifm of the famous Mr *James Melvil*, in the anfwer to that queftion, What is Faith ? *Anf.* ' It is my *fure be-* ' *lief* that God baith may and will fave *me* in the blood of Jefus ' Chrift, becaufe he is Almighty, and has promifed fae to do.'

And it muft be obferved, that the real agreement and harmony between the more *ancient* and *later* way of defcribing faith, is declared, by the Acts of Affembly 1647 and 1648, receiving and

approving

approving the *Westminster* Confeffion and Catechifms, in which
it is exprefsly afferted, *That the faid Confeffion and Catechifms are
in nothing contrary to the received doctrine of this Church :* Which
they would not have faid, if they had not thought, that the de-
fining of faith, by a receiving and refting upon Chrift alone for falvation, as he is offered to us in the gofpel, did imply that fiduci-
al act or *appropriating* perfuafion, whereby they ordinarily defcribed
faith before that time. However, our *Confeffion* and *Catechifms* are
clear enough upon this head, Conf. chap. xiv. fect. 3. ' Faith is
' different in degrees, weak or ftrong,——growing up in many to
' the attainment of a *full affurance*, through Chrift :' *(N. B.* Faith
is here afferted to differ in many, not as to *affurance*, but as to the
fulnefs of affurance) and here they cite *Heb.* vi. 11. and x. 22.
which Scriptures fpeak of the affurance of *faith*, and not of *fenfe.*
Larger Cat. queft. 72. ' Juftifying faith is a faving grace, wrought
' in the heart of a finner, by the Spirit and word of God, where-
' by he—not only affenteth to the truth of the promife of the
' gofpel, but *receiveth* and *refteth* upon Chrift and his righteouf-
' nefs, therein held forth, for pardon of fin, and for the accepting
' and accounting of HIS Perfon righteous in the fight of God for
' falvation.' Which they found on *Philip.* iii. 9. and *Acts* xv. 11.
queft. 73. ' Faith juftifies a finner——only as it is an inftrument,
' by which he *receiveth* and *applieth* Chrift and his righteoufnefs.'
Queft. 170.——' By faith they receive and apply unto *themfelves*
' Chrift crucified, and all the benefits of his death.' Queft. 189.
' The preface of the Lord's prayer (contained in thefe words, *Our*
' *Father which art in Heaven)* teacheth us, when we pray, to draw
' near to God with confidence of his fatherly goodnefs, and OUR in-
' tereft therein.' And *Shorter Cat.* queft. 86. ' Faith in Jefus Chrift
' is a faving grace, whereby we receive, and reft upon him alone for
' falvation, as he is offered TO US in the gofpel.' Where it is
evident, that though the offer TO US be mentioned *laft*, yet it is
to be believed *firft.*

    Wherefore, the Prefbytery *did,* and *hereby do acknowledge, de-
clare* and *affert,* That, in juftifying faith, there is a real perfuafion
in the heart of a finner, that *Chrift is his ;* that *he fhall have life
and falvation by him ;* and that *whatfoever Chrift did for the redemption of mankind, he did it for him ;* upon the foundation and
ground of the gift or promife of Chrift in the gofpel that is made
to finners of *Adam's* family, *as fuch ;* and fo, there is in it a refting
upon him alone for the whole of this falvation.

    And the Prefbytery do hereby *reject* and *condemn,* for the above
reafons, the following doctrines taught in the forefaid Acts of Affembly ; (1.) That faving and juftifying faith *is not* a perfuafion
in the heart, that Chrift is ours ; that we fhall have life and falvation by him ; and that whatever Chrift did for the redemption
of mankind, he did it for us : (2.) That *all* the perfuafion in juftifying faith, is only *a belief and perfuafion of the mercy of God in
Chrift, and of Chrift's ability and willingnefs to fave all that come*
                                                  unto

unto him; this being fuch a faith as *Papifts* and *Arminians* can fub-
fcribe unto, in a confiftency with their other errors and herefies :
(3.) That one muft *firft* come to Chrift and be a true believer, *be-*
fore he appropriate Chrift and the whole of his˙ falvation to himfelf,
upon Scripture ground and warrant ; whereby the true nature of
faving faith is fubverted : All which tenets and opinions are contrary to the *Word of God*, and the above paffages of our *Confeffion*
and *Catechifms.*

A R T I C L E III. [Of the Injury done to the Doctrine of Grace,
under the head of *Holinefs not neceffary to Salvation.*]

Under the odious title of *Holinefs not neceffary to Salvation,*—The
Affembly 1720 cites the *Marrow* from page 150 to page 153, to
prove the Author's erroneous opinion (as they allege) *viz.* That
holinefs is not neceffary to falvation. But the Author is in thefe pages
fhewing, that the believer is altogether delivered from the law as a
Covenant of Works; which appears from the Author's own words,
in anfwer to the queftion of *Neophytus, How far forth* am I *delivered*
from the law, as it is the Covenant of Works? *Evangelifta* anfwers,
‘ As it is the Covenant of Works, you are *wholly* and *altogether* de-
‘ livered and fet free from it ; you are dead to *it,* and it is dead to
‘ *you.*—You are now under another covenant, to wit, the *Covenant*
‘ *of Grace,* and you cannot be under *two* covenants at once, neither
‘ wholly nor partly ; and therefore as, before you believed, you
‘ were wholly under the *Covenant of Works, as Adam* left both you
‘ and all his pofterity, after his fall ; fo now, fince you have be-
‘ lieved, you are wholly under the *Covenant of Grace.*—You are
‘ now fet free, both from the commanding and condemning power
‘ of the *Covenant of Works.*——And therefore, though hereafter
‘ you do through frailty tranfgrefs any of all the *ten Commandments,*
‘ yet do you not thereby tranfgrefs the *Covenant of Works ;* there is
‘ no fuch covenant now betwixt *God* and *you.*’ Which doctrine of
the believer's freedom from the Law as a Covenant of Works, is
fo far from *denying* that holinefs is neceffary to falvation, that it
eftablifhes the neceffity thereof in its own place, as fhall be made
evident in confidering the paffages which are quoted by the Affembly 1720, upon this head, in order to fix upon the Author that erroneous opinion, That *holinefs is not neceffary to Salvation,* viz.
p. 153. ‘ If the law fay, good works muft be done, and the command-
‘ ment muft be kept, if thou wilt obtain falvation ; then anfwer
‘ you and fay, *I am already faved before thou cameft; therefore I*
‘ *have no need of thy prefence,*——*Chrift is my Righteoufnefs, my*
‘ *Treafure and my work. I confefs, O law, that I am neither godly*
‘ *nor righteous, but yet this I am fure of, that he is godly and righte-*
‘ *ous for me,* page 185. Good works may rather be called a be-
‘ liever's *walking* in the way of eternal happinefs, than the *way* it-
‘ felf.’ The judgment of the Affembly is as follows, ‘ This Doc-
‘ trine tends to flacken people's diligence in the ſtudy of holinefs,
‘ contrary

' contrary to *Heb.* xii. 14. 2 *Thess.* ii. 13. *Ephes.* ii. 10. *Isa.* xxxv.
' 8. *James* ii. 10. *Confess.* chap. xiii. § 1. *Larger Cat.* Quest. 32.
' *Confess.* chap. xv. § 2.'

The General Assembly 1722 allege, that the above passage,
p. 153. ' Will plainly bear (the Author's) rejecting of the law, as it
' requires good works to be done (by a justified person) and the
' commandments to be kept, in order to obtain salvation ; which
' (say they) is further strengthened by the following words (the
' omitting whereof by the Assembly is complained of in the repre-
' sentation) viz. *For in Christ I have all things at once, neither need*
' *I any thing more that is necessary unto salvation.* Then, personal
' holiness and good works, and perseverance in holy obedience to
' the law of God, are not (in the Author's opinion) necessary unto
' salvation ; and a man may have all things necessary to salvation,
' though he be not yet a godly man : And therefore the Assem-
' bly have given no just ground of quarrel ; seeing, though good
' works be excluded from being the ground of justification, yet they
' are necessary in the justified, in order to their obtaining the en-
' joyment of eternal salvation.' And to the same purpose, they
speak in vindication of the 8th act of Assembly 1720, enjoining ministers to preach the doctrine *of free justification through*
our blessed Surety, the Lord Jesus Christ, received by faith alone ;
and of the necessity of an holy life, in order to the obtaining of ever-
lasting happiness. In which recommendation, as the *imputation of*
Christ's righteousness unto us is omitted ; so, as the said Act stands
in connection with the 5th, condemning the believer's plea of
Christ's *active obedience,* in answer to the Law's demand of *good*
works for obtaining salvation, it seems evidently to favour the erroneous doctrine, of something *wrought in,* or *done* by the sinner,
as his righteousness, in keeping the *new* and gospel law. Accordingly the Assembly 1722, upon this head say, ' If they quarrel the
' phrase, *of obtaining everlasting happiness,* they may also quarrel the
' Apostle's expression, 1 *Cor.* ix. 24, 25. and *Phil.* iii. 11, 12. For it
' relates to the obtaining of *enjoyment* and *possession,* and not of *right*
' and *title* to everlasting happiness, which all justified persons have
' already attained.' And in the same act they assert, that it is of
dangerous tendency to teach, ' That the law acknowledgeth no
' works for obtaining salvation, but *such* as found a title to it be-
' fore the Lord : Whereas (say they) the law requires good works
' in order to the *obtaining salvation,* though they do not found a
' title to it.'

The plain scope and tendency of all this, is to countenance and
pave the way for the *Arminian* and *Baxterian* doctrine,—of the *gos-*
pel its being a new, proper, preceptive *law* with sanction, binding
to *faith, repentance,* and other duties, which are consequential
to the entrance of sin, and the revelation of the grace of God in the
gospel ; our personal obedience to which is necessary for our *ob-*
taining everlasting happiness : And though the Assembly owns that
the righteousness of Christ founds our *title ;* yet, according to them,

we

we ourſelves are to work for the *poſſeſſion;* as will further appear from the expreſs words of the aɛt of Aſſembly 1722. ' The Aſſem-
' bly conſidering, that there have at this time been publiſhed ſeve-
' ral poſitions and expreſſions, of a pernicious and dangerous ten-
' dency ; ſuch as, [That in the *goſpel*, properly ſo taken, there are
' no *precepts*, the commands of faith and repentance not excepted ;
' that holy obedience is not properly a *federal* or *conditional mean*,
' nor has any kind of *cauſality*, in order to the obtaining of glory.']
Where it is obvious,

1ſt, That the Aſſembly holds it as a truth, that, in the *goſpel*, properly ſo taken, there are *precepts*, and that the commands of faith and repentance are among that number. —— If the goſpel be taken *largely*, for a ſyſtem of all the Doɛtrines, Promiſes, Pre-cepts, Threatnings, and Hiſtories, which any way concern man's recovery and ſalvation ; then, no doubt, *all* the precepts which belong to, or are deducible from the law of the ten Command-ments, are contained in it ; many of which precepts, having a manifeſt conneɛtion with the entrance of ſin, could not be promulgated before the goſpel was revealed, ſuch as, *Faith, Re-pentance, witneſſing for Truth, and againſt the defeɛtions of the times,* and the like : But then, *all* theſe precepts are reducible to the Law of the *ten Commandments*, though they had no due and proper objeɛts, nor occaſion of being exerciſed in an innocent ſtate. And therefore, if the goſpel is taken *ſtriɛtly* and properly, as it is contr diſtinɛt from the Law, it is a *promiſe*, containing glad tidings of a Saviour, with Grace, Mercy, and Salvation in him, to loſt ſinners of *Adam*'s fa-mily ; according to *Gen.* iii. 15. " I will put enmity between thee
" and the woman, and between thy ſeed and her ſeed ; it ſhall
" bruiſe thy head, and thou ſhalt bruiſe his heel. *Iſa.* lxi. 1, 2, 3.
" The ſpirit of the Lord God is upon me, becauſe the Lord hath
" anointed me to preach good tidings unto the meek ; he hath ſent
" me to bind up the broken-hearted, to proclaim liberty to the
" captives, and the opening of the priſon to them that are bound;
" To proclaim the acceptable year of the Lord, and the day of
" vengeance of our God ; to comfort all that mourn ; to appoint
" unto them that mourn in *Zion*, to give unto them beauty
" for aſhes, the oil of joy for mourning, the garment of praiſe for
" the ſpirit of heavineſs ; that they might be called trees of righte-
" ouſneſs, the planting of the Lord, that he might be glorified.
" *Luke* ii. 10, 11. Behold, I bring you good tidings of great joy,
" which ſhall be to all people ; for unto you is born this day, in
" the city of *David*, a Saviour, which is Chriſt the Lord. *Rom.* x.
" 15.——— How beautiful are the feet of them that preach the go-
" ſpel of peace, and bring glad tidings of good things. *Gal.* iii. 8.
" The Scripture foreſeeing that God would juſtify the Heathen
" through faith, preached before the goſpel unto *Abraham*, ſaying,
" In thee ſhall all nations be bleſſed." And thus, when the goſpel is taken in its *proper* ſenſe, there are *no* precepts in the goſpel, and conſequently *all* precepts (theſe of Faith and Repentance not ex-
E   cepted)

cepted) belong to the *Law;* which, according to the nature of it, being a perfeƈt and complete rule of all internal as well as external ob: dience, muſt faſten the *new duty* upon us, the ſame moment that the goſpel reveals the *new objeƈt.* For it is evident, that, by the law of creation, or of the ten Commandments, given to *Adam* in paradiſe in the form of a Covenant of Works, *Adam* was bound to believe whatever God *ſhould reveal,* and obey whatever he *ſhould command;* ſo that there never was nor can be an inſtance of duty, owing by the creature to the Creator, that is not commanded in the moral Law, either *expreſsly* or by neceſſary *conſequence.* And there-fore, ſince the Lord was pleaſed to reveal his grace and good-will in the goſpel, *Faith* and *Repentance* are required in the Law, as well as other good works, according to the doƈtrine held forth from the Scriptures in *Larger Catechiſm,* queſt. 104. where, among the duties required in the *firſt* Commandment, we find, ‘ Believing him, truſt-‘ ing, hoping, delighting and rejoicing in him,——being careful in ‘ all things to pleaſe him, and ſorrowful when in any thing he is ‘ offended, and walking humbly with him.’ And queſt. 105. a-mong the ſins forbidden there are, ‘ Miſbelief, diſtruſt, incorrigible-‘ neſs and hardneſs of heart,’ or impenitency, according to the Scrip-ture there quoted, Rom. ii. 5. *But, after thy hardneſs and impenitent heart, treaſureſt up to thyſelf wrath.*

Beſides, if the *Law* does not bind ſinners to believe and repent, then Faith and Repentance, conſidered as works, would enter into the ground of our *juſtification* before God : For the Scripture con-ſiders all works properly done by us, as works of the *Law,* and, un-der *that* charaƈter, excludes them from the ground of our juſtification in the ſight of God ; wherefore if Faith and Repentance are not works of the *Law,* they are not excluded from, but muſt belong to the ground of our *pardon* and *acceptance.* And this doƈtrine is the foundation of the *Neonomian* error, which eſtabliſhes the neceſ-ſity of another righteouſneſs, agreeable to a *new goſpel Law,* in our own perſons, beſides the righteouſneſs of Chriſt, as the imme-diate ground of our *acceptance* and *confidence* before God : And it evidently lands in the *Pelagian* univerſal grace ; for if there be a new Law, which was never given to *Adam* in innocency, *Adam* never loſt that grace whereby that new Law is to be obeyed ; and if ſo, he who gave that Law, according to them, behoved in juſtice to give new *univerſal grace* wherewith to obey it.

2dly, In conſequence of the above doƈtrine, of precepts in the goſpel properly ſo taken, the ſaid aƈt of Aſſembly maintains, that holy obedience is properly a *federal or conditional mean,* and *has ſome kind of cauſality,* in order to the obtaining of glory. It can-not but be matter of the deepeſt humiliation to all the true lovers of Zion, that ever ſuch doƈtrine ſhould be inculcate by the authori-ty of the General Aſſembly of the Church of *Scotland,* whereby ſo wide a door is opened to *Arminian* and *Socinian* errors, which, like a flood, have overflown this Church and land.

This Preſbytery do cordially acknowledge and maintain the *ne-ceſſity*

cessity of holinefs and good works, in their proper place : That they
are *neceffary*, as an acknowledgment of God's Sovereignty, and in
obedience to his command, and as being the end of our election,
redemption, and effectual calling ; *neceffary*, as a part of that falvation, which is begun here, and perfected hereafter ; *neceffary*, as
being expreffions of our gratitude, and as being a fpecial defign of
Word and Ordinances ; that they are *neceffary*, for making our calling and election fure : And, as is contained in our Confeffion of
Faith, chap. xvi. § 2.—' Good works done in obedience to God's
' commandments, are the fruits and evidences of a true and lively
' faith ; and by them believers manifeft their thankfulnefs, ftrength-
' en their affurance, edify their brethren, adorn the profeffion of the
' gofpel, ftop the mouths of the adverfaries, and glorify God.' But,
as the Author of the *Marrow* nowhere denies, but elfewhere plainly afferts, the *neceffity* of holinefs in the above or like refpects (the
fore-mentioned paffages, condemned by the Affembly, having a manifeft relation to the believer's plea againft the Law's demands of perfect perfonal obedience ;) fo, from the whole tenor of the Affembly's act, it is obvious, that they want to bring in our own holinefs or
good works, as having a *caufal influence* upon our eternal falvation,
and as a *federal* and *conditional* mean thereof; which tends to over-
throw the whole Scripture-doctrine of *complete* righteoufnefs and
falvation, *only* in and through Jefus Chrift our Lord.

Nor will it vindicate the Affembly, that they fpeak of *obtaining
the enjoyment and poffeffion* of everlafting happinefs by a holy life,
but not a *right and title* to it, which they allow that all juftified
perfons have already attained. For the further clearing of which
matter it would be confidered, that,

1. The condemned paffages of the *Marrow* on this head, fpeak
not of falvation *completed*, or everlafting happinefs in heaven, but
of falvation *commenced*, or begun on earth : For, in oppofition to the
Law, as a Covenant of Works, demanding works to obtain falvation, the Author brings in the believer anfwering, *I am faved already by the works and obedience of another ;* meaning *falvation begun*, according to *Eph.* ii. 8, 9. *By grace are ye faved, not of works.*
2 *Tim.* i. 9. *He hath faved us,—not according to our works.* Tit.
iii. 5. *Not by works of righteoufnefs which we have done, but according to his mercy he faved us :* And hence the Spirit of God (2 *Tim.*
ii. 10. 1 *Pet.* i. 9.) declares that believers, even in *this life*, receive
the end of their faith, the falvation of their fouls, *and obtain the falvation which is in Chrift Jefus.* All thefe, and many other places
of Scripture, fpeak as the Author does, of falvation obtained *already*
in this life : For, (as is declared, 1 *John* iii. 36.) *He that believeth on
the Son hath everlafting life,* viz. in the beginnings and firft fruits
of it upon earth, as well as the title to it. Now furely we hold
our right to, and *poffeffion* of this begun falvation, not by *our works*
or holy life, but by *grace*, as it reigns through the righteoufnefs of
Jefus Chrift unto eternal life : Yet this part of the *Marrow*, fpeaking in fuch a ftrain, is condemned by the forefaid act of Affembly :
while

While the Affembly's reftricting the term *falvation*, unto the *complete* enjoyment of falvation, is plainly for the fake of that dangerous principle, That though our faith and good works are not meritorious, or the caufe of our *juftification*, yet they are the caufe of our *eternal falvation*, and a federal and conditional mean thereof. Thus,

2. Whereas the forefaid act of Affembly declares, That the obtaining of everlafting happinefs is to be meant of the obtaining the *enjoyment* and *poffeffion* thereof, and not of a *right* and *title* thereto ; it will follow, in a confiftence with this Act, that it is found doctrine to teach, That we obtain the *right* to heaven and eternal life by Chrift's doing and obedience, but we obtain the *poffeffion* of it by our own doing or perfonal holinefs : But the Scripture afferts, 1 *Theff.* v. 9. that we *obtain falvation by our Lord Jefus Chrift.* Eph. i. 11. *In whom alfo we have obtained an inheritance.* Heb. ix. 12. He hath *obtained eternal redemption for us.* And whereas that Scripture, 1 *Cor.* ix. 24. quoted by the Affembly, feems to make the incorruptible crown to be *obtained* by our running; it is to be remarked, that the meaning can never be of the believer's obtaining, not by *faith*, but by *works ;* for that word in the original fignifies to *receive* or apprehend, and fo it is rendered in the words immediately preceding, *viz. One receiveth the prize*, and thus, *So run that ye may obtain*, is, fo run that ye may *receive* the crown ; which indeed agrees with the Scripture-notion of heaven, as it is a gift freely beftowed upon the ground of Chrift's righteoufnefs, *Rom.* vi. ult. *The gift of God is eternal life, through Jefus Chrift our Lord.* Luke xii. 32. *It is your Father's good pleafure to give you the kingdom.* And, as eternal life is freely given of God, fo it is dearly purchafed by Chrift ; and not only the *right* and *title* to it, but alfo the *poffeffion* of it is purchafed, and therefore called the *purchafed poffeffion,* Eph. i. 14. of which we have the *earneft* in this life, that is not only a pledge, but part in hand.

Now, fince both part and whole, the begun and complete poffeffion are purchafed and obtained by the blood of Chrift : Who that underftands the gofpel will venture to fay of any of them, that they are obtained by *our works* or holy life, as properly a *federal* and *conditional* mean ? Though without holinefs none fhall fee God, nor can any be partakers of the inheritance of the faints in light, who are not made meet for it by fanctification and holinefs of heart, and (in adult perfons) of life alfo, this being a great part of that falvation whereof they are here poffeffed, being alfo neceffarily connected with, and preparative unto the full poffeffion of eternal life hereafter :) Yet, to fpeak in the terms of the forefaid act, teaching that we are to *obtain* the poffeffion of eternal life in heaven by our works and holy life, and, at the fame time, condemning the expreffion of being faved *already* by the works and obedience of Chrift, is far from having the appearance of orthodoxy. And at beft, what ftrange divinity would it be in heaven, to fay, Though we cannot boaft that we have obtained a *right* to
heaven,

heaven, yet we have obtained the *possession* of it by our holy life; our title to this salvation we now enjoy, was obtained by *Christ's obedience*, but our possession of it was obtained by our own obedience! This language would sound ill in heaven, and consequently it should sound ill on earth; for it is not the joyful sound of the gospel, but the unpleasant sound of life, as it were by the works of the law: Whereas we find in Scripture, that the language of the redeemed is, and will be through eternity, *Salvation to our God, which sitteth upon the throne, and unto the Lamb*, Rev. vii. 10. and chap. v. 9.——*Thou wast slain, and, hast redeemed us unto God by thy blood*, &c.

As to the above passages of the *Marrow* condemned by the Assembly, *viz.* ' I am already saved *before thou camest*, therefore I have no
' need of thy presence; for in Christ I have all things at once,
' neither need I any thing more that is necessary to salvation;
' Christ is my righteousness, my treasure, and my work. I con-
' fess, O Law, that I am neither godly nor righteous, but yet this
' I am sure of, that he is godly and righteous *for me*.' These being the words of the great reformer *Martin Luther*, wherein he expresses the perfection and extent of Christ's active obedience in our room, answering both the *godliness* and the *righteousness* required in the law, and answering the law charge against the believer, as being neither *godly* nor *righteous* in himself, and in the eye of the law; were never before quarrelled or condemned by any *Protestant* Church. Indeed, as the believer has no plea, in answer to the law's demand of satisfaction to justice for sin, but the sufferings of Jesus Christ our Surety; so he has no plea, in answer to the law's demand of *perfect obedience*, for entitling him to eternal life and salvation, but *that* which here stands condemned by the Assembly. For the law demands of every person a *nature* perfectly innocent and holy, while demanding a *life* perfectly righteous; and, since we have neither the *one* nor the *other* in ourselves, we must have them *both* in Christ, else we must remain under the condemnation of the law: Wherefore, as there is a *personal* holiness of nature, and righteousness of life, begun in every true believer, which shall be carried on and perfected in the work of sanctification; so there is in Christ a perfect, complete holiness of *nature* and righteousness of *life*, which is *imputed* to the sinner, in the moment of believing, for his justification in the sight of God; and consequently [CHRIST IS GODLY AND RIGHTEOUS FOR ME] is the only answer that the believer can give to the law's demand of good works to be done, and keeping the commandments for obtaining salvation; according to *Rom.* iv. 5. *To him that worketh not, but believeth on him that justifieth the ungodly, his faith is counted for righteousness.* 1 Cor. i. 30. *But of him are ye in Christ Jesus, who of God is made unto us wisdom, and righteousness, and sanctification, and redemption.* And *Confess.* chap. xi. ŷ 1.
' These whom God effectually calleth, he also freely justifieth:—
' Not for any thing wrought in them, or done by them;—but by
                                                          ' imputing

' imputing the obedience and satisfaction of Christ unto them.'
So that, if we have recourse in the least to our personal holinefs,
as the ground, in whole or in part, of our *enjoyment* of grace here,
or glory hereafter, we dishonour both the law and Lawgiver,
and *rival* it with the Son of God, by seeking to divide the glory
of our salvation with him.　And now, whereas the act of Assembly above considered teaches the necessity of personal holinefs and
obedience, *as a federal and conditional mean, and as having some
kind of causality in order to the obtaining of glory*, it effectually *cuts
off* the believer's plea, of the perfect righteousnefs of Christ and
holinefs of his nature, imputed to the believer, in answer to the
law's demand of a holy nature and perfect righteousnefs of life,
for justification and title to eternal life.　And as this is contrary
to our own *Confession of Faith*, so likewise to the doctrine of other
reformed　Churches, particularly, *Palatine* Catechism, ' *Quest.*
' How art thou righteous before God?　*Anf.*——The perfect *satis-*
' *faction, righteousnefs* and *holinefs* of Christ, is imputed and given
' unto me, as if I had neither committed any sin, neither were
' any blot or corruption cleaving unto me:—Not only the per-
' fect *righteousnefs*, but even the *holinefs* of Christ also is imputed
' and given unto me:—The satisfaction, righteousnefs and holi-
' nefs of Christ alone, is *my righteousnefs* in the sight of God.'
　Wherefore, the Prefbytery *do hereby declare and affert* (1.) That
the *gospel*, properly and strictly taken, as contradistinct from the
law, is a *promise* containing glad tidings of a Saviour, with grace,
mercy and salvation in him, to lost sinners of *Adam*'s family;
and confequently, *all precepts* (these of faith and repentance not
excepted) do in a strict and proper sense belong to the *law*.
(2.) That, as the *suffering* of Jefus Christ our Surety, is the believer's only plea, in answer to the law's demand of *satisfaction*
to justice;　so the complete and perfect conformity of the Surety
to the law, in *nature* and *life*, is the believer's only plea, in answer
to the law's demand of *perfect obedience*.
　And the Prefbytery *did*, and *hereby do*, upon the above grounds,
condemn the following *tenets* and *opinions*, (1.) That the *gospel* strictly taken, is a new, proper and preceptive *law* with sanction, binding to faith, repentance, and the other duties which are confequen-
tial to the revelation of the grace of God.　(2.) That though the
righteousnefs of *Christ* only founds our *title* to eternal glory; yet
it is our *personal* holinefs, or our own obedience to the new law,
upon which we obtain the *possession* thereof.　(3.) That our perfonal holinefs or good works have a *causal influence* upon our eternal salvation, and are a *federal* and *conditional* mean thereof; in
which fenfe, the Assembly's directing ministers to preach the neceffity of an holy life, in order to the obtaining of everlasting happinefs, is of very dangerous confequence to the doctrine of *free
grace*.　All which positions are contrary to the *Scriptures* and
paffages of our *Confession* of Faith and Larger *Catechism* above-cited.

ARTICLE

ARTICLE IV. [Of the Injury done to the Doctrine of Grace, under the head of] *Fear of Punishment, and Hope of Reward, not allowed to be motives of a Believer's Obedience.*

Under this head, the following passage is cited by the Assembly, for proof of this their charge against the Author of the *Marrow,* *viz.* page 181. ' Would you not have believers to eschew evil, and ' do good for fear of hell, or hope of heaven ? *Anf. No indeed,* ' ——for so far forth as they do so, their obedience is but *slavish.*' And the Assembly add, That ' a great deal more to this purpose is ' to be seen, *pages* 175, 179, 180, 182, 183, 184. and appears con- ' trary to *Psal.* xlv. 11. *Psal.* cxix. 4, 6. *Exod.* xx. 2. *James* i. 25. ' and ii. 8, 10, 11, 12. 1 *Tim.* iv. 8. *Col.* iii. 24. *Heb.* xi. 6, 26. ' *Rev.* ii. 10. 2 *Cor.* v. 9, 10, 11. *Heb.* xii. 2, 28, 29. 2 *Pet.* iii. 14. ' *Conf. chap.* xvi. § 2. and 6.' Moreover, the Assembly, *anno* 1722, say (in answer to the Representation given in the former year by twelve brethren) ' This part of the Assembly's act (*viz.* ' 1720) is unfairly represented, seeing they do not draw that infe- ' rence (*viz.* fear of punishment and hope of reward, not allowed ' to be motives of a believer's obedience) from that passage a- ' lone, but cite other passages, as page 175. and 179, where for ' fear of punishment and hope of reward, in express terms, and in ' general without exception, are removed from being motives unto ' the believer's obedience. To which (they say) may be added, ' page 73. where he says of believers under the Old Testament, ' *That answerably as they believed, answerably they yielded obedience* ' *to the Law, without fear of punishment, or hope of reward.* And ' page 216. cited in the following paragraph of the act, where he ' exhorts the believer, *to yield free obedience, without having respect* ' *either to what the Law of works either promiseth or threateneth ;* ' *but also, without having respect to what the Law of Christ either* ' *promiseth or threateneth.* And the Assembly further complain of ' the brethren, That, when they say, they heartily approve of the ' Author's position in this sense, viz. *That believers are not to do good* ' *for hope of obtaining heaven by their own works and doings,* (which ' (say the Assembly) is a calumnious insinuation against the ortho- ' dox doctrine) they do not declare themselves, whether they allow ' that a believer may and ought to be moved unto obedience by ' the hope of heaven, in any other sense, than that of a hope of ob- ' taining a right and title to it by his own works ; or if no regard ' can be had to the promised reward of the heavenly inheritance ' by a believer in his obedience, without its being mercenary.' But here it may be observed, that the Assembly do not treat the brethren fairly, while they take no notice of what is said in the an- swer given in to the Commission of the former Assembly, unto the question put to them on this head ; wherein they shew their agree- ment in principle with the Scriptures and Confession of Faith, and

with

with renowned orthodox Divines, as to the motives of the believer's obedience : Whereas the Assembly do insinuate, in the challenge here given, as if there were ground to suspect the brethren of mantaining, That *no regard can be had to the promised reward of the heavenly inheritance, by a believer in his obedience, without its being mercenary ;* while yet the brethren have in their answer to the 12th *Query,* among other things, declared, ' That taking heaven for a state of ' endless felicity, in the enjoyment of God in Christ, we are so far ' from thinking that this is to be excluded from being a motive of ' the believer's obedience, that we think it the *chief end* of man ' next to the glory of God ---- and this indeed the believer is to ' have in *his eye* as the recompence of reward, and a noble *motive* ' of obedience.'

What the doctrine delivered by the Author of the *Marrow,* upon this head, amounts to, may be clearly seen from the pages quoted by the Assembly, and is plainly this ; That *legal mercenary* hopes, ought not to influence the believer's obedience, on the one hand ; nor *servile, slavish, legal* fears, on the other : Or that, on the one hand, the believer is not to seek to be influenced to obedience, by the fear of his falling under the *eternal loss* of the favour of God, and under his *eternal displeasure* in hell-fire, contrary to that unalterable state of favour into which the believer is brought ; neither is he to fear that even *temporal punishment* shall be inflicted upon him, in a way of *vindictive wrath ;* both which are unsuitable to that full assurance of faith of the Lord's unchangeable love, and of a saving inviolable relation to him, which the believer is always called to maintain and hold fast with stedfastness : And, on the other hand, That believers are not to be influenced to obedience by the hope of reward, or hope of Heaven as the reward *any way due* to their obedience ; that is, either *purchased* or *procured,* or to be *obtained,* by any works of righteousness done by them, and so a reward of *debt,* as if their works were either meritorious in *themselves,* or meritorious by *paction,* which is inconsistent with the whole method of grace revealed in the gospel, and particularly to the lively faith believers are called to maintain, of their obtaining Heaven and Glory, even the full possession of eternal life, by *grace* or *free gift,* and not by works.

As to what the *law of Christ* promiseth or threatens, it is plain, the scope of the Author of the *Marrow* is, That, though the believer is called to expect to share of the *discipline* of his Father's family in the case of transgression, and to entertain a deep sense of the awfulness of his Father's *frowns* and *rods ;* yet is he called more and more to grow in the genuine spirit and disposition of the children of God, so as to have the *love* of his Father more and more the motive of his obedience, rather than the *fear* of the rod : Even as a child, though called to fear his father's displeasure, yet is called to study more and more to be impressed with a sense of his father's love ; so as he may be excited and influenced in his obedience by the love of his father, and not the fear of the whip.

That

That this is the declared meaning of the Author, is plain from thefe paffages quoted, and other places in the book : Particularly, after it is faid page 174. ' We do not therefore deftroy or condemn ' the law, becaufe we fay it doth not juftify :' Then page 175, *Neophytus* is brought in fpeaking, ' I do now in fome fmall mea- ' fure believe, that I am by Chrift freely and fully *juftified and ac-* ' *quitted from all my fins,* and *therefore* have no need either to ef- ' chew evil or do good for fear of punifhment or hope of reward.' Again, the like expreffion, which the Affembly points to page 179. ftands thus in connection : page 178. at the clofe, ' Before a man ' do truly believe in Chrift he may fo reform his life, &c.—Yet ' being under the Covenant of Works, all the obedience that he ' yields to the law——is (page 179.) of—the *bond woman,*—— ' works of a *bond-fervant,* that is moved and conftrained to do all ' that he doth for fear of *punifhment* and hope of *reward.*——He ' pretends the ferving of *God,* whereas indeed he intends the fer- ' ving of *himfelf,*——is an empty vine, and therefore muft needs ' bring forth fruit to himfelf.——When a man, through the hear- ' ing of faith, has received the Spirit of Chrift, *Gal.* iii. 2. that ' Spirit, (page 180.) according to the meafure of faith, writes the ' lively law of love in his heart, whereby he is enabled to work ' freely,—without the coaction or compulfion of the law ;—— ' the love of Chrift——carries him on,——*freely* and *chearfully,* ' ——to keep the law, without fear of hell or hope of heaven.'

Thefe and the like paffages, plainly fhew, that the Author's fcope is to guard againft a *mercenary fervile fpirit* in our obedience, act- ing or bringing forth fruit to ourfelves. And to ftretch the Au- thor's words *further,* as if they imported a direction or exhortation to difregard the awfulnefs of the Divine threatenings and judg- ments againft fin, exciting to ftand in awe of committing it ; and the excellency of the recompence of reward, fo as not to be there- by animated in the obedience of love ; is contrary to the plain in- tent of the Author's reafoning. As, particularly, may be obferved in his doctrine concerning the believer's reward, that it is in God himfelf, even in the enjoyment of him who is the reward and in- heritance : And that this reward is not the reward of *fervice* done by the believer ; and fo not the reward of *fervants,* but the inheri- tance of *fons,* fecured to the believer, previous and without all re- fpect had to his obedience as the price in whole or in part, or any federal condition of the poffeffion of it : So that he ought to have this reward continually in his eye, to animate him in running for- ward to the full poffeffion ; not to obtain it, as the hire or reward of his running, but to haften to it, becaufe it is *freely made over* unto him. And thus, confequently, as the believer ought to have in his eye the depth of that *mifery* he has by grace efcaped ; and to re- gard and deeply confider the *threatenings* of that eternal wrath and mifery, as they difcover what even his fins in themfelves deferve ; that he may be thereby excited to adore the love of his Redeemer, in delivering him from fo great a death, and to thankful obedience

F to

to him for the same, according to 2 *Cor.* v. 14, 15. So the believer is also bound to lay to heart the threatenings of *fatherly chastisements*, as they are evidences of his heavenly Father's detestation of sin, exciting him to abhor it the more ; and likewise as evidences of his Father's love in *correcting him for his profit*, and declaring he will do so, that he may be a *partaker of his holiness.*

Such views as these, the believer is called to take of what is promised and threatened. Nevertheless, it is quite another matter, and contrary to the genuine exercise of the Christian as such, to be influenced by the promise and threatening ; as if his obedience were the *procuring cause, or proper federal ground or condition* of his freedom from the punishment, and enjoyment of the blessing : Seeing all *boasting* is excluded by the gospel ; so that the believer's sole and only plea is the *free, sovereign* mercy of God in Christ. Thus, the ground of expectation before God, or of confidence in his sight (which is what the Author of the *Marrow* has evidently in view) is surely not our obedience, either to the *Law of works* or the *Law of Christ :* And therefore, the motive to obedience ought not to be any *servile respect* (which is evidently what the Author points to) either to what the *Law of Works* or the *Law of Christ*, either promiseth or threateneth.

But, as the Assembly condemn the expressions used in the *Marrow*, without any distinction ; so by what they say in their act, they give too evident ground to think, it is in the above-declared view and sense of the words that they condemn them as erroneous ; and that it is the scope and design of their act, to assert a believer's duty of yielding obedience, from a principle and upon the motives of *legal, servile* fears and hopes.

That this is the mind of the Assembly, is evident ; considering, That under this same head, p. 22, 23, 24. of their act 1722, they allow no other legal servile hope of heaven, but the hope of obtaining a right and title to it by our own works ; insinuating that no other regard to the reward in our obedience, can be reckoned *mercenary* : And they assert, that the hope of obtaining the *possession* and *enjoyment* of heaven, by our obedience, is not mercenary.

This then, being the end the Assembly do assign unto the obedience of believers, *viz.* That it is in order to their *obtaining* eternal life ; their after doctrine in this act 1722, page 26. shews, That hereby they understand, that the holy obedience of believers is properly a *federal* and *conditional mean and cause* of their enjoying that eternal life : And thus, they divide the glory of our enjoying salvation between Christ and the creature, as to the *ground* of the hope thereof ; while they plainly say, that believers are to be influenced in obedience by these hopes of heaven, which are, at least in part, to be *founded* upon their own obedience, as the proper federal condition thereof ; whereby the whole gospel is perverted, and another foundation laid, than that which God has laid in *Zion* : And this doctrine is particularly contrary to these Scriptures *Tit.* iii. 4, 5, 6, 7. " But after that the kindness and love of God our " Saviour toward men appeared, not by works of righteousness

" which

" which we have done, but according to his mercy he faved us, by
" the wafhing of regeneration, and renewing of the Holy Ghoft;
" which he fhed on us abundantly, through Jefus Chrift our Sa-
" viour : That being juftified by his grace, we fhould be made
" heirs according to the hope of eternal life. *Rom.* iv. 4, 5, 16.
" Now to him that worketh, is the reward not reckoned of grace,
" but of debt : But to him that worketh not, but believeth on him
" that juftifieth the ungodly, his faith is counted for righteoufnefs.
" Therefore it is of faith, that it might be by grace ; to the end
" the promife might be fure to all the feed. And chap. vi. 23.
" The wages of fin is death : But the gift of God is eternal life,
" through Jefus Chrift our Lord. Chap. v. 21. That as fin hath
" reigned unto death, even fo might grace reign through righteouf-
" nefs unto eternal life, by Jefus Chrift our Lord. Chap. xi. 6.
" and if by grace, then is it no more of works; otherwife grace is
" no more grace : But, if it be of works, then is it no more grace;
" otherwife work is no more work. *Gal.* iii. 3, 11, 12, 13, 14.
" Are ye fo foolifh ? Having begun in the fpirit, are ye now made
" perfect by the flefh ? But that no man is juftified by the law in the
" fight of God, it is evident : For, the juft fhall live by faith. And
" the law is not of faith : But the man that doth them fhall live in
" them. Chrift hath redeemed us from the curfe of the law, being
" made a curfe for us : For it is written, curfed is every one that
" hangeth on a tree : That the bleffing of Abraham might come
" on the Gentiles through Jefus Chrift ; that we might receive the
" promife of the Spirit through faith. Chap. v. 4, 5. Chrift is be-
" come of no effect unto you, whofoever of you are juftified by the
" law ; ye are fallen from grace. For we through the Spirit wait
" for the hope of righteoufnefs by faith. 2 *Tim.* i. 9. Who hath
" faved us, and called us, with an holy calling : not according to
" our works, but according to his own purpofe and grace, which
" was given us in Chrift Jefus, before the world began. *Eph.* ii.
" 9, 10. Not of works left any man fhould boaft : For we are his
" workmanfhip, created in Chrift Jefus unto good works, which
" God hath before ordained that we fhould walk in them. *Luke*
" xvii. 10. So likewife ye, when ye fhall have done all thefe
" things which are commanded you, fay, We are unprofitable fer-
" vants : We have done that which was our duty to do. *Luke* i.
" 74, 75. That he would grant unto us, that we being delivered
" out of the hands of our enemies, might ferve him without fear,
" in holinefs and righteoufnefs before him, all the days of our life :"
And to our *Confeffion of Faith*, chap. xii. ' All thofe that are
' juftified, God vouchfafeth,————to make partakers of the
' grace of adoption : *By which* they——inherit the promifes, as
' heirs of everlafting falvation. Chap. xiv. § 2.——The principal
' acts of faving faith are, accepting, receiving, and refting upon
' Chrift alone for——*eternal life, by virtue of the covenant of grace,*'
comparing the Scripture-proof there adduced, *Acts* xv. 11. *But we
believe, that through the grace of the Lord Jefus Chrift we fhall be*
SAVED,

SAVED, *even as they. Conf.* chap, xx. fect. 1. ' The liberty which
' Christ hath purchafed for believers, confifts in——their yielding
' obedience unto him, not out of *flavish fear*, but a *child-like love*
' and willing mind.'

From thefe and the like Scriptures and paffages of the Confeffion
it evidently appears, That true fpiritual obedience flows from, and
is influenced by faith's view of the love of Chrift; cafting out that
fear of wrath and punifhment which neceffarily hath torment in it;
" 1 *John* iv. 18. There is no fear in love; but perfect love cafteth
" out fear: Becaufe fear hath torment.' Verfe 19. We love him
" becaufe he firft loved us. *Pfal.* xxvi. 3. Thy loving kindnefs is
" before mine eyes: And I have walked in thy truth :" And,
that on the other hand, it is not influenced by any *fervile legal hope*
of reward, or any view of a *legal* or *federal* connection between the
obedience and the enjoyment or poffeffion of the inheritance, which is
by promife alone. Neither is there the leaft countenance given to
the oppofite doctrines, by thefe Scriptures, where the everlafting inheritance is expreffed under the notion or by the title of reward;
feeing this reward (being infinite) can only be purchafed by an infinite price, even that price given by *Emmanuel :* And this reward
is declared to be given to us, not of *debt*, but of *grace*; not to him
that worketh, but to him that worketh not, but believeth on him
that juftifieth the ungodly; and to be the gift of God through Jefus
Chrift our Lord. Thus, the believer, in his refpect to this recompence of reward, is called to act, not for life as the reward of *his*
fervice, but from the faith of his certain enjoyment of that life as
the reward of the fervice of the *new Covenant-head ;* and the more
he thus views it, the more fhould and will he be animated to cheer-
ful obedience.

Wherefore the Prefbytery, for the neceffary vindication of truth,
manifeftly injured by the faid acts of Affembly, *did*, and *hereby do*,
affert, maintain and *declare*,

1. That it is a precious gofpel-truth, That believers, being heirs
of the heavenly inheritance, and having it not by the law, but by
free promife, through Jefus Chrift; ought not to be influenced in
their obedience, by the hopes of obtaining the poffeffion and enjoyment of the inheritance, by any works, of righteoufnefs or obedience *done by them*.

2. That, as they fhould be moved to obedience from the confideration of the excellency of the heavenly inheritance, even of
God in Chrift as their inheritance and exceeding great reward,
and by many other motives; fo, particularly, they are to be
influenced by this motive, That they have got the begun poffeffion of this inheritance, and have the full poffeffion thereof fecured,
by *rich grace* and *free promife*, through Jefus Chrift; being made
heirs of God, and joint-heirs with Chrift.

3. That, though the believer ought to entertain an holy awe
and dread of the majefty of God, and of the awfulnefs of his
threatenings and judgments, both temporal and eternal, againft fin

and

and finners; and to confider from them what even *his* fins in them-felves. deferve : Yet, he is not called to be moved or excited to obedience to the precepts of the law (either as it is a Covenant of Works, or as it is a Rule of Life) by the *fear* of his falling into hell, for omitting duty or committing fin : But is ever called fully to believe his infallible fecurity from going down into that pit, through the ranfom which God has found out ; fo as through the firm and lively faith of this his fafety in a ftate of favour with God, to have his heart more and more filled with that *love* which cafteth out tormenting fear, and will be natively exercifed in chearful gofpel-obedience to all the Lord's commandments.

4. That, though believers fhould remember and ferioufly con-fider, that there is *difcipline* in their Father's family ; and believe that *they* may expect it, when they tranfgrefs his law, and keep not his commandments :. Yet, as this difcipline is inftituted on account of *remaining corruption* in them ; fo, the confideration thereof ought to excite them more and more to improve the blood of Jefus Chrift by faith, for *draining* and *mortifying* this corruption ; and particu-larly, for fubduing and removing the *legal bias* and difpofition, which is the ftrength of fin in them ; that thus, they may be more and more made to ferve in *newnefs of fpirit*, and not in the *old-nefs of the letter*.

And the Prefbytery *do*, in like manner, *condemn* the following pofitions, as *dangerous, unfound* and *erroneous :*

1. That there is a *legal connection* inftituted, between the obe-dience of believers, and their enjoying rewards, with efcaping pu-nifhments, temporal or eternal; or, that the Lord deals with them in this matter upon *Law terms ;* and that their hopes of enjoying the one, and efcaping the other, are to rife and fall according to the meafure of *their* obedience.

2. That a perfon's being moved to obedience by the hope of heaven, cannot be faid to be *mercenary*, in any other fenfe than that of a hope of obtaining a *right* and *title* to it, by his own works : And, that a believer ought to be moved to obedience, or, to ef-chew evil and do good, by the hopes of his enjoying heaven, or any good temporal or eternal, by his own obedience, as the *federal, conditional* mean, and *caufe* thereof.——All which pofitions are contrary to the above-cited, and many other Scriptures and paf-fages in our ftandards.

ARTICLE V. [Of the injury done to the Doctrine of Grace,] under this Head, *That the Believer is not under the Law as a Rule of Life.*

The Affembly 1720, attempting to prove againft the Author of the *Marrow*, his maintaining the forefaid error, *viz. That the believer is not under the Law as a Rule of Life*, relate fome paffages out of his book, and then cite a number of pages. The paffages related are three; the laft whereof, together with the pages only cited, not being again repeated in the Act 1722, we fhall confider

them

them in the *first* place. The third paffage then in *act* 1720, is taken from p. 216. of the book, *viz.* ' You will yield obedience to
' the law of Chrift, not only without having refpect to what the
' *law of works* either promifeth or threatneth; but alfo without
' having refpect to what the *law of Chrift* either promifeth or
' threateneth : And this is to ferve the Lord *without fear of any pe-*
' *nalty* which either the law of works or the law of Chrift threatens.
' *Luke* i. 74.' This being the paffage that affords the Affembly
the moft plaufible pretence for charging the Author with maintaining, *That the believer is not under the law as a rule of life*, it is
eafy to fee how ftraitened they were to prove their point, and how
impracticable it was for them to do fo, without doing injury to
truth. For this paffage relates not properly to *obedience*, but to
the *motives* of the believer's obedience; and fo it belongs to, and
is noticed upon another head. But, as here it is adduced to prove,
that the Author *denies* the believer to be under the law as a *rule
of life*, it feems to be very far from anfwering that end. For,
in the paffage itfelf, the Author is owning, that the believer fhould
yield obedience to the law : And though it could be proven, that
he is unduly cutting off all regard to the *promife* or *threatening ;*
yet, while he is not rejecting the *command*, but maintaining the
regard the believer ought to have thereunto, and owning the obligation he is under to yield obedience; the faid paffage will never
prove his maintaining that the believer *is not* under the law as a
rule of life, but the quite contrary; fince here his fcope is not to
fpeak of the *law*, but the *fanction*, and to fhew what a pure regard the believer ought to have to the *command*, though *promifes*
and *threatenings* both were cut off, and confequently to the law itfelf, as a *rule of life*. But the wrong done to the *Author*, by attempting (though in vain) to prove the forefaid error againft him,
were the lefs to be noticed, if, at the fame time, the moft precious
gofpel-truths were not wronged and wounded, as appeareth in what
follows.

The Affembly 1720, on the fame head, cite pages 5, 153, 180,
156, 157, 163, 199, 209, 210, of the *Marrow*, as alfo proving
againft the Author, his denying the law to be a *rule of life*
to the believer; and both there, and in the clofe of the Act, they
condemn thefe paffages, as contrary to the holy Scriptures, and our
Confeffion of Faith. But, as it would be tedious, and is needlefs,
to repeat here the paffages contained in thefe pages ; fo, any that
pleafe to confult them, may not only fee how egregioufly the
Author is wronged by that Act, but alfo may be filled with aftonifh-
ment to behold, how far the General Affembly of the Church of
Scotland has been left of God, to condemn fo many *precious truths,*
manifeftly founded on the Word of God, and moft agreeable to
our Confeffion of Faith and Catechifms.

But farther, the Affembly 1720, pretending to prove againft
the Author of the *Marrow*, his maintaining the forefaid error, viz.
That the believer is not under the law as a rule of life ; are fo far
from

from doing it, that, for proof, they cite and condemn these words, page 250. *As the law is the Covenant of Works, you are wholly and altogether set free from it ;* and page 151. *You are now set free both from the commanding and condemning power of the Covenant of Works.* These words, says the Assembly 1722, ' are con-
' descended upon as a part of the proof against the Author, of his
' maintaining this erroneous tenet, *That the believer is not under*
' *the law as a rule of life ;*' and then they declare, ' that it was
' not the meaning nor intention of the said *Act*, in the least to in-
' sinuate, that *Believers in Christ are under the law as a Covenant of*
' *Works,* or that they are obliged to seek justification by their own
' obedience.——And, the Assembly appoints, *that these two* (fore-
' said) *passages shall not be understood as a proof of the foresaid er-*
' *ror, in any other sense,* than as, the Assembly did apprehend, that
' the Author understood by the *Covenant of Works, the Moral Law*
' *strictly and properly taken,* as it appears he does (say they) in
' other places of the book ; as particularly, page 7. he says, *That*
' *indeed the law of works signifies the Moral Law ; and the Moral Law*
' *strictly and properly taken, signifies the Covenant of Works.*' Now,
the injury which by all this is done to truth, appears in the following particulars :

(1.) They find fault with the *Marrow* for asserting, that the *Moral Law* is strictly and properly the *Covenant of Works*, and that *as such,* the believer is wholly and altogether set free from it ; as if his speaking in this manner did afford any proof of his maintaining that the believer is not under the law as a *rule of life :* Where-
as, in our *Larger* Catechism, quest. 93. What is the *Moral Law ?* The answer given is a strict and proper definition of the *Covenant of Works,* from which the said Catechism, in answer to quest. 97. asserts, that believers are delivered, *so as thereby they are neither justified nor condemned ;* which is the same, in other words, with their being neither under the command of it to be justified, nor under the threatening of it to be condemned thereby. Hence, the Assembly by that *act,* instead of fixing the foresaid *error* upon the Author of the *Marrow,* have but further condemned the *truth* as expressed both in that book and in our *Catechism ;* pretending that the gospel-doctrine, delivered in that strain, tends some way or other to loosenes, or to loose the believer from his obligation to the law as a *rule of life.*

(2.) As they charge an erroneous sense upon the *Marrow,* without being able to prove it ; so, their own wrong sense and erroneous opinion upon this matter, is too evident in that *act ;* as there-
in they make these two propositions to be *one* and the *same,* viz. *That believers in Christ are not under the Law as a Covenant of Works,* and, *That they are not obliged to seek justification by their own obedience.* These two propositions they make alternatives, and of the same import : But, if they be the same, then the believer is no otherwise freed from the Covenant of Works after he is a *believer,* than he was before when in *unbelief ;* for *then,* he was as little obliged to
seek

feek juftification by his own obedience, as he is *now* ; and confe-quently, he was as much delivered from the Law as a Covenant of Works, *before* he believed as *fince*. Yea, according to this errone-ous pofition, the *believer* is no more delivered from the Law, as a Covenant of Works, than the *unbeliever*, who is as little obliged to feek juftification by his own obedience as the believer is. Here then is a grofs perverting of the truth, relating to the command of the Law as a *Covenant of Works ;* of which our leffer Catechifm fpeaks in this manrier, *When God created man, he entered into a Co-venant of Life with him, upon condition of perfect obedience* : For, inftead of this, the form of that Covenant is altered by the faid act of Affembly, from man's being obliged to *perfect obedience*, which was the condition of that Covenant, and of life by it, to his being obliged to *feek life and juftification* by his obedience ; which is not at all the proper form of the Covenant of Works, but a confe-quence from it, and fuch, as the Covenant of Works might have been fulfilled without regarding it. For, by *feeking*, here muft be underftood either *aiming at*, or *claiming* juftification by our own obedience : But now, if *Adam* had performed that perfect obedi-ence therein required, he would have been juftified, though he had never fought or aimed at his own *juftification* by it, but merely aimed at the *glory of God* his creator ; and though he was to have life by or for his obedience, yet he could never feek or *claim* life and juftification by it, *till once* he had performed it perfectly.

So dangerous then, is the altering the words of our ftandards by any fuch untenable glofs, that this in particular will be found full of grofs error. For, if believers in Chrift their *not being un-der the Law as a Covenant of Works*, is the very fame with their *not being obliged to feek juftification by their own obedience ;* it will plainly follow, that *all the children of men* now, efpecially fuch as are under the outward difpenfation of the gofpel, are delivered from the command of the Law as a Covenant of Works, equally with the *believer*, becaufe none of them are obliged to feek juftification by their own obedience : And if they be not under the *command* of the Covenant of Works, how can they be under the *curfe* of it ? Where no *Law* is, there is no *tranfgreffion*, and where no *tranfgref-fion*, there is no *penalty :* Moreover, where none of thefe are, there is no need of *Chrift's obedience*, either active or paffive in their room, and fo no need of a *preached gofpel :* This *new way* then which the Affembly takes to explain the *old truth*, tends to deftroy both Law and Gofpel. But it is plain, that though the Law or Covenant of Works be a *broken*, yet it is a perpetually *binding* Law ; and though the finner be an *infolvent* debtor, yet the debt, both of obedience and fatisfaction, *lies upon his head*, as long as he is under the Law, and not under Grace, through union to Chrift the fecond *Adam*, who came to pay that double debt ; from which believers in Chrift are alone free, through the imputation of his Law-fulfilling and Ju-ftice-fatisfying Righteoufnefs unto them.

The

The proper form of the *commanding* power of the Law, as a Covenant of Works, lies in the connection between *perfonal obedience*
and *eternal life:* And this connection ftill ftands in that Law under
which the unbeliever keeps himfelf by his unbelief; which therefore ftill binds him, both under the forfeiture of *life* which the Law
promifed, and under an obligation, to that *obedience* which had this
life promifed to it.   This keeps all the lapfed race of *Adam* under an obligation, not to feek juftification by their own obedience, but to defpair of life and juftification by the Law, and to
expect death and condemnation by it, according to the fentence
thereof paffed againft them, *Gal.* iii. 10.   This ftanding connection between *obedience and life,* and *difobedience and death,* in
that Law of Works which they are under, holds them prifon-
ers to the Law and Juftice of God, as long as their debt to both
is not paid.   This *connection* then, makes the unbeliever ftill lie
under the condemning power and curfe of the Law ; whereas, if he were not ftill under the *precept,* he could not be under the
penalty of that Covenant.   This alfo makes him need to feek
life and juftification by the obedience of Chrift ; for, if he were
not under the forefaid binding obligation of the Law, both as
to the DO and DIE of it, *he would not need* to feek juftification
to life, nor falvation from death, by the doing and dying, the obedience and fatisfaction of *Jefus Chrift.*   But, the act of Affembly
1722, does fo much cloud and darken this truth, that it plainly fup-
pofes *none* are under the Law as a Covenant of Works, *except thefe*
that are under an obligation to feek juftification by their own obedience : And this being an obligation *none at all* are under, whether
believers or unbelievers, the common and valuable privilege of *all*
the hearers of the gofpel, in their being obliged to feek juftification
only through the obedience and fatisfaction of Jefus Chrift, is thus
quite *fubverted,* and at the fame time, the great diftinguifhing privilege of *believers,* in being not under the *Law* but under *Grace,* is
by this act, quite *overthrown* and turned to *nothing.*
The faid Affembly owns, in their act, that it is a precious gofpel-truth, *That believers are free from the Law as it is a Covenant of*
Works: And hence, fome may allege that it is a ftrained confe-
quence, from their alternative, viz. *That they are not obliged to feek*
juftification by their own obedience, to infer their deftroying the believer's privilege, and making him no happier than the unbeliever.
But, that their meaning is not wrefted, is plain from their condemning, in the *fame* act the following pofition, viz. *That the Law, as to*
believers, is really divefted of its promife of life and threatening of
death : For hence it is evident, that they keep the *believer* both under the commanding and condemning power of the Law, equally
with the *unbeliever:* Becaufe if the Law, as to the believer, be not
really divefted of its *Promife of eternal life;* then the believer is
under the *commanding* power thereof, fo that his obedience as fuch,
hath the promife of life: An thus, he muft have another Law-title
to life and eternal falvation, th n Chrift's obedience.   And, if the
Law, as to the believer, be not really divefted of its *threatening of*

death; then, the believer is under the *condemning* power thereof, so as his sin and disobedience, even after he is in a justified state, brings him under a legal obnoxiousness to eternal death : Wherefore, by his obedience he must have a right to life and justification, according to the Law ; and by his disobedience, he must come under condemnation and death, according tot he same Law : And consequently, he is not at all delivered from the Law as a *Covenant of Works;* so as to be thereby neither justified nor condemned : Which is directly contradictory, both to the Scriptures of truth, and to our Confession of Faith and Catechisms.

This doctrine is not only highly injurious to the revelation of the grace of God, concerning the believer's privilege ; but it is also dishonouring and discrediting to the righteousness of Christ our Surety : While, notwithstanding his *doing,* upon which alone the believer's legal title to eternal life stands, and his *dying,* upon which alone his legal security from eternal death stands ; yet, the believer, by this corrupt doctrine, is kept both under the DO and DIE of the Covenant of Works : Under the DO, because the Law hath still the promise of life, even as to him, and the DIE, because the Law hath still the threatening of death, even as to him : And so he hath neither legal security for life by Christ's doing, nor legal security against death by Christ's dying. Thus, by this act of Assembly, the believer is condemned to remain still under that old Law, *If thou doest, thou shalt live,* and, *if thou doest not, thou shalt die ;* notwithstanding all that Christ hath done and suffered for him.

It will not salve the matter that the Assembly adds, after the foresaid condemnatory words, these following, viz. *If by the Law they understand the Moral Law, the Rule of Life.* For as this, when connected with the foresaid condemned position, seems *unintelligible ;* so, if it have any meaning at all, it must import their making the Moral Law, as it is a *Rule of Life* to the believer, to have a *promise of life* and a *threatening of death ;* or to be a Law giving life to them upon their obedience, and denouncing death and damnation to them upon their disobedience : Which seems a turning the Gospel to a Law ; or the Law, as a *Rule of Life* in the hand of Christ, to a Law or *Covenant of Works,* speaking life to the doer, and death to the transgressor : And so the matter comes still to the same issue, though they would seem here to explain what they condemn.

And that the believer, according to the Assembly, is still kept under the Law, as a *Covenant of Works,* will further appear, if it is considered ; that, though they seem to deny, that believers in Christ are under the Law as a Covenant of Works ; yet, while they assert, that the Law as a Rule of Life, which the believer is under, is a Law that is not divested of *a promise of life,* and *a threatening of death,* (which, according to our Confession, is the proper notion of the Law, as a Covenant of Works;) they likewise maintain, that holy obedience is properly a *federal* or *conditional mean,* and has some kind of *causality,* in order to the obtaining of glory : From which

which it plainly follows, that believers are still kept under the *Covenant of Works;* in regard that, according to them, the believer's obedience has still the promise of life, and his disobedience the threatening of death; and in regard they likewise make their holy obedience to be properly a federal or conditional mean, in order to their obtaining eternal glory. But, whatever Law they will have the believer under, as a Law of life or death, it is plain that the believer is under *no such Law ;* seeing, as the Apostle says, Gal. iii. 18, 21, 22. *If the inheritance be of the Law, it is no more of promise——For, if there had been a Law given which could have given life, verily righteousness should have been by the Law : But the Scripture hath concluded all under sin ; that the promise, by faith of Jesus Christ, might be given to them that believe.*

Therefore the Presbytery *did,* and *hereby do, acknowledge, affert and declare,* in opposition to these foresaid acts of Assembly 1720, and 1722, upon this head :

(1.) That, whatever the Law, as a Covenant of Works, promiseth or threatens, in itself, and as to them that are under it ; yet the Law, as to the believer, is really *divested of the promise of life and threatening of death :* And that the believer holds his legal right and claim to eternal life, only by the perfect *obedience of Christ* to the Law in his room; and his legal security from eternal death, only by the complete *Satisfaction of Christ* to the Justice of God, in the threatening of the Law ; and not by any Law having promise of life to his own obedience, or threatening of death to his disobedience : For, *where sin abounded, grace did much more abound ; that as sin hath reigned unto death, even so might grace reign through righteousness unto eternal life, by Jesus Christ our Lord,* Rom. v. 20, 21.

(2.) That, as the Moral Law doth for ever bind all, as well justified persons as others, to the obedience thereof : So, to assert that the Moral Law, strictly and properly considered, as a Covenant of Works, is what *the believer is wholly and altogether set free from,* will never prove against the asserter thereof, that he maintains the believer is not under the Law as a *Rule of Life.* And, to the same purpose, the Presbytery maintain, That as the Law is a Covenant of Works, believers are *wholly and altogether set free from it,* set free both from the *commanding* and *condemning* power thereof ; or, as our Larger Catechism expresses it, *delivered from the Moral Law as a Covenant of Works, so as thereby they are neither justified nor condemned :* And that, from the maintaining of this truth, it will no ways follow, that the believer is not under the Law as a *rule of life.*

(3.) That, though it be the duty of all who hear the gospel, to seek after life and justification by the obedience of Christ, and not by their own ; yet, while through unbelief they do not so, they remain under the Law as a *Covenant of Works,* both in its *commanding* and *condemning* power ; and that it is the peculiar privilege of *true believers in Christ,* to be free therefrom.

(4.) That, though *all unbelievers* do remain under the Law as a Covenant of Works, both in its commanding and condemning power; yet *none of them* are obliged to feek juftification by their own obedience; but on the contrary, it is the great duty of all the hearers of the gofpel, and alfo their ineftimable privilege, to feek juftification *only* through the obedience and fatisfaction of Chrift.

And the Prefbytery do hereby likewife *condemn* thefe following *pofitions*, which are countenanced by the forefaid acts of Affembly upon this head.

(1.) That the doctrine of the believer's being freed from the Law as a Covenant of Works, whether in its commanding or condemning power, is a doctrine of *licentioufnefs*; tending any way to free the believer from obligation to the Law, as it is a *rule of life. Do we make void the law through faith? God forbid; yea, we eftablifh the law.*

(2.) That the believer his *not being under the Law*, and his *not being obliged to feek life by his own obedience*, are propofitions of the fame import; as if *unbelievers*, under a gofpel-difpenfation, were *equally* free from the commanding power of the Law, as a Covenant of Works, with *believers*; fince they are not obliged to feek juftification by their own obedience any more than believers. The Prefbytery, therefore *condemn* this doctrine, as highly prejudicial to the truth relating both to the *Law*, and the *Gofpel*; and to the *diftinguifhing privilege* of the believer in Chrift, his being not under the *Law* but under *Grace*.

(3.) That the Law, as to believers, is vefted with a *promife of life* and *threatening of death*; fo as their obedience is properly a *federal or conditional mean*, in order to their obtaining eternal glory.

(4.) That unbelievers, in their being under the Law as a Covenant of Works, are obliged to feek juftification by their own obedience.——All which pofitions are injurious to truth, and oppofite to the Scriptures and our Confeffion of Faith and Catechifms.

ARTICLE VI. Concerning the Injury done to the Doctrine of Grace; under the Head of (what the Affembly calls) *The fix Antinomian Paradoxes.*

The Affembly, in their aforefaid act, *anno* 1720, condemn the diftinction which the Author of the *Marrow* makes ufe of, for ridding marches between the ftate of an *unbeliever*, who is condemned already by the fentence of the broken Law, and the ftate of a *believer*, for whom there is no condemnation; and for fhewing, in what fenfe the believer in Chrift is *bound to obey the Law*, and in what fenfe he is *delivered from it.*

The Author, for this purpofe, diftinguifheth between the Law as it is the *Law of Works*, which he explains to be the Law confidered as a Covenant of Works; and the Law as it is the *Law of Chrift*, by which he underftands the Law confidered as a rule of obedience in

in the hand of Chrift, who hath as their Surety, fulfilled the righteoufnefs of the Law, as a Covenant, in their room and ftead.

For what reafon the Affembly condemns this diftinction, it is
hard to conceive. Can it be thought, that an Affembly of the
Church of *Scotland*, denies any difference between the Law as a Covenant *of Works*, and the Law as a *Rule of Duty?* If this foundation
be deftroyed, What can the righteous do, who falleth feven times a-
day? For, according to this doctrine, when he falls into any, even
the leaft fin, he falls under, and becomes liable unto the heavy fentence of the Law of Works, *Curfed is every one that continueth not
in all things written in the book of Law to do them.* The reafon is
plain, becaufe, according to the Affembly's act, the Law, even
with refpect to the believer, ftill retains its *Covenant-form;* contrary to Scripture, *Rom.* vi. 14. *Rom.* vii. 2, 3, 4. and to the Confeffion of Faith, chap. xix. § 6.

The Affembly, in the condemnation of this diftinction, do, *fim-
pliciter*, condemn fix propofitions, called by them, *Antinomian Paradoxes;* the moft of which are the exprefs words of the Holy
Ghoft in Scripture, and fo muft needs have a found fenfe. If the
Affembly had dealt with that candour, which might have been expected from a court of Chrift, they would have told in what fenfe
the Author *admits*, and in what fenfe he *rejects* thefe propofitions :
But, feeing the Affembly has neglected this, it is proper to take a
view thereof in the words of the Author, pages 198, 199, 200,
201, 202, 203.

There, *Neophytus* craves of *Evangelifta*, his judgment concerning the following propofitions : (1.) *That a believer is not under
the Law, but is altogether delivered from it;* (2.) *That a believer
doth not commit fin;* (3.) *That the Lord can fee no fin in a believer;*
(4.) *That the Lord is not angry with a believer for his fins;* (5.)
That the Lord doth not chaftife a believer for his fins; (6.) *That a
believer hath no caufe, neither to confefs his fins, nor to crave pardon
at the hands of God for them; neither yet to faft, nor mourn, nor
humble himfelf before the Lord for them.*

Unto this *Evangelifta* anfwers, in the words following ; ' Thefe
' points, which you have now mentioned, have occafioned many need-
' lefs and fruitlefs difputes ; ——for, in one fenfe, they may all of
' them be *truly affirmed;* and, in another fenfe, they may all of
' them be *truly denied.* Wherefore, if we would clearly underftand
' the truth, we muft diftinguifh betwixt the Law as it is the *Law
' of Works*, and as it is the *Law of Chrift*. Now, as it is the *Law
' of Works*, it may be *truly* faid, That a believer is not under the
' Law, but is delivered from it, according to that of the Apoftle,
' *Rom.* vi. 14. *Ye are not under the Law, but under Grace;* and
' *Rom.* vii. 6. *But now we are delivered from the Law.* And if
' believers be not under the Law, but are delivered from the Law,
' as it is a *Law of Works*, then, though they fin, yet do they not tranf-
' grefs the *Law of Works;* For *where no Law is, there is no tranf-
' greffion, Rom.* iv. 15. And therefore, faith the Apoftle *John*, *Who-
' foever*

' foever abideth in him sinneth not, 1 *John* iii. 6. that is (as I con-
' ceive) whosoever abideth in Christ by faith, sinneth not against
' the *Law of Works.* And, if a believer sin not against the *Law*
' *of Works*, then can God see no sin in a believer, as a transgression
' of *that Law*; and therefore it is said, *Numb.* xxiii. 21. *He hath*
' *not beheld iniquity in* Jacob, *neither hath he seen perverseness in*
' Israel. And again it is said, *Jer.* l. 20. *At that time the iniquity*
' *of* Israel *shall be sought for, and there shall be none; and the sins of*
' Judah, *and they shall not be found:* And in *Cant.* iv. 7. Christ
' saith concerning his Spouse, *Behold thou art all fair, my Love;*
' *and there is no spot in thee.* And if God can see no sin in a be-
' liever, then assuredly he is neither *angry*, nor doth *chastise* a be-
' liever for his sins, as a transgression of *that Law* : And hence it
' is, that the Lord saith, concerning his own people, that were be-
' lievers, *Isa.* xxvii. 4. *Anger is not in me;* and again *Isa.* liv. 9.
' the Lord speaking comfortably to his Spouse the Church, saith,
' *As I have sworn, that the waters of* Noah *shall no more go over*
' *the earth ; so have I sworn, that I will no more be wroth with thee,*
' *nor rebuke thee.* Now, if the Lord be not angry with a believer,
' neither doth chastise him for his sins, as they are any transgression
' of the *Law of Works;* then hath a believer neither need to *con-*
' *fess* his sins unto God, nor to *crave pardon* for them, nor yet to
' *fast* nor *mourn*, nor *humble* himself for them, *as* conceiving them
' to be any transgression of the Law, as it is the *Law of Works.*
' Thus, you see, that if you consider the Law in this sense, then all
' these points follow; according as you say our friend *Antinomista*
' hath endeavoured to persuade you.
' But if you do consider the Law, as it is the *Law of Christ*, then
' they do not so, but quite *contrary.* For, as the Law is the *Law*
' *of Christ*, it may be *truly* said, that a believer is under the Law,
' and not delivered from it, according to that of the Apostle, 1 *Cor.*
' ix. 21. *Being not without Law to God, but under the Law to Christ;*
' and according to that of the same Apostle, *Rom.* iii. 31. *Do we*
' *then make void the Law through faith ? God forbid; yea,* (by faith)
' *we establish the Law.* And if a believer be under the Law, and
' not delivered from it, as it is the Law of Christ; then, if he sin,
' he doth thereby transgress the *Law of Christ :* And hence I do
' conceive it is, that the Apostle *John* saith, both concerning him-
' self and other believers, 1 *John* i. 8. *If we say we have no sin, we*
' *deceive ourselves, and the truth is not in us :* And so saith the A-
' postle *James*, chap. iii. 2. *In many things we offend all.* And if
' a believer transgress the Law of *Christ*, then doubtless, *he* seeth
' it ; for it is said, *Prov.* v. 21. That *the ways of man are before the*
' *eyes of the Lord, and he pondereth all his goings:* And in *Heb.* iv. 13.
' it is said, *All things are naked and opened unto the eyes of him with*
' *whom we have to do.* And if the Lord doth see the sins that a
' believer doth commit against the Law, as it is the Law of Christ,
' then doubtless, he is *angry* with them ; for it is said, *Psal.* cvi. 40.
' That because the people *went a whoring after their own inventions,*
' *there-*

' therefore was the wrath of the Lord kindled against his people, in so
' much that he abhorred his own inheritance: And in Deut. i. 37.
' *Moses* faith concerning himself, *The Lord was angry with him.*
' And if the Lord be angry with a believer for his tranfgreffing the
' Law of Chrift, then affuredly (if need be) he will *chaftife* him
' for it ; for, it is faid, concerning the feed and children of Jefus
' Chrift, *If they forfake my Law, and walk not in my judgments,*
' *then will I vifit their tranfgreffions with the rod, and their iniqui-*
' *ties with ftripes :* And, in 1 *Cor.* xi. 30. it is faid, concerning be-
' lievers, *for this caufe* (namely their unworthy receiving of the
' Sacrament) *many are weak and fickly among you, and many fleep.*
' And if the Lord be angry with believers, and do chaftife them
' for their fins, as they are a tranfgreffion of the Law of Chrift ;
' then hath a believer caufe to *confefs* his fins unto the Lord, and
' to *crave pardon* for them ; yea, and to *faft*, and *mourn* and *hum-*
' *ble* himfelf for them, as conceiving them to be a tranfgreffion of
' the *Law of Chrift.*'

From the above quotation it is plain, like a fun-beam, in what
fenfe the fix propofitions called *Antinomian*, are either *true* or *falfe*,
according to the Author ; and how neceffary the above diftinction,
of the Law into the *Law of Works* and the *Law of Chrift*, is, for
clearing the true fenfe of the above propofitions, which are moftly
fcriptural. But, the Affembly, by condemning the above diftinction, have overclouded many precious truths ; which cannot mifs
to iffue in a jumbling *Law* and *Gofpel* together, and the bringing
of believers under a fpirit of *bondage unto fear*, from which they
are delivered by the grace and fpirit of the gofpel.

Neither have the Affembly, in their explicatory act, 1722, offered any thing of moment, either for the clearing up of truth, or
for their own neceffary vindication ; as will appear if we confider,
(1.) That the Author of the *Marrow*, page 267, cited by the act of
Affembly 1722, page 23, head vi. is there fpeaking of the diftinction betwixt *Law* and *Gofpel* ftrictly taken, both which have their
proper ufes, even to the believer ; but he is not fpeaking one word
of the believer's not being, in any fenfe, under the *Law of Works*,
or of his being under any Law. (2.) The Affembly, in their faid
act, 1722, for their own exoneration, fay, that the Affembly 1720,
do only condemn the above diftinction of the Law, into the Law of
Works and the Law of Chrift, *as it is applied by the Author*, (viz.
of the *Marrow*,) for defending the fix *Antinomian* Paradoxes : From
whence it neceffarily follows, that thefe fix points of doctrine are
condemned by the Affembly, *according to the fenfe* put upon them,
by the Author's applying to them that diftinction of the Law, into
the *Law of Works*, and the *Law of Chrift* ; or, as the Author explains himfelf, the Law as a *Covenant* and the Law as a *Rule of Obedience.* And thus, thefe following precious truths of the everlafting
Gofpel, lie buried under the *condemnatory* fentence of the General
Affembly of this National Church, for above twenty years back-
ward.

1st, That believers are not under the Law as a *Covenant*, but are altogether freed from it ; though they are still under it as a *Rule of Obedience.*

2dly, That a believer doth not commit sin, as it is a transgression of the *Law of Works ;* but, when he sins, he transgresseth the Law, considered as a *Rule of Holiness* in the hand of a Mediator.

3dly, That God sees no sin in a justified believer, under the covert of the perfect righteousness of Christ, as a transgression of the *Law of Works ;* though he still sees and marks it, as a transgression of the *Law of Christ.*

4thly, That the Lord is not angry with a believer for his sins, with a *vindictive wrath ;* but with a *fatherly displeasure.*

5thly, That the Lord doth not chastise a believer for his sins, as an implacable enemy, with *Law-vengeance ;* but with the *rod of a Father*, not for their destruction but for their reformation.

6thly, That though the sins of believers, considered as transgressions of the *Law* or *Covenant of Works*, do deserve eternal death ; and though they are even many ways aggravated above the sins of others : Yet, seeing their sins, considered as transgressions of the *Law* or *Covenant of Works*, were *laid over upon Christ ;* therefore a believer, when he *fasts* and *mourns* for, and *confesseth* his sins, ought to view them as laid over upon the Surety, purging away their guilt by his blood : And, in the faith of remission and forgiveness through the righteousness of Christ, and of his deliverance from the commanding and condemning power of the Law of Works, thereby ; he is to *fast* and *mourn* for, and *confess* his sins, as to his concern with them in his justified estate, not as violations of the Law of Works, but only as *violations of the Law in the hand of a Mediator*, and, as committed against, and dishonouring unto his *reconciled* God and Father in Christ.

Thus, by the doctrine of the foresaid act, the foundation of all evangelical obedience is *overturned,*—the wells of Salvation, out of which we should draw water with joy, are *stopt ;* and we are *sent back* to the Law as a Covenant, to seek righteousness, life and comfort. Wherefore, in order to clear and maintain the foundations of gospel-obedience, and the springs of the believer's consolation ; the Presbytery *did*, and hereby *do, acknowledge, assert and declare,*

1st, That the distinction, as explained in the *Marrow*, is good and scriptural, *viz.* That there is a wide difference between the Law as a *Covenant of Works*, and the Law as a *Rule of holy Obedience.*

2dly, That a believer in Christ, is neither under the commanding nor condemning power of the Law, as a *Covenant of Works ;* although he be still under the Law as a *Rule of Obedience* in the hand of a Mediator.

3dly, That God seeth not iniquity in *Jacob*, or in true believers, as it is a transgression of the *Covenant of Works ;* but only, as it is a transgression of the Law in the *hand of Christ*, who bore our sins in his own body on the tree.

4*thly*, That though the elect, by nature, be children of wrath even as others ; yet, through the death and satisfaction of Christ, the Lord's *vindictive anger* is turned away from, *fury* is not in him against any soul that is come to the blood of sprinkling : And yet, he may and will be angry with his dear children, so as to visit their *iniquity with the rod*, and their *transgressions with stripes ;* but, because he will not take his love from *Christ*, nor break his covenant with *him*, therefore not with *them*, who are his seed.

5*thly*, That when a believer *fasts*, mourns for and *confesseth* his sins, he ought not to do it in a *legal* way, as one standing under a *Covenant of Works*, either as to its precept or penalty ; but he ought to do it with the hand of faith upon the head of the great Sacrifice and Atonement, as one whose person and duties *are accepted* in the Beloved : And thus he ought to *fast, mourn* for and *confess* his sins, before his *reconciled* God and Father ; believing that God, according to his promise, is merciful to his unrighteousness, and will remember his sins no more.

Moreover, the Presbytery *did*, and hereby *do, condemn* and *reject* the following erroneous and dangerous *positions*, taught by the Assembly :

1*st*, That *believers* are under the Law, and not altogether freed from it, as a *Covenant of Works*.

2*dly*, That, when a believer sins, he sins against the *Law of Works*, and therefore must be liable to the *penalty* thereof.

3*dly*, That God seeth iniquity in believers, as it is a violation of the old *Covenant of Works*, made with *Adam* in innocency ; and consequently, that he sees it with an eye of *vindictive justice ;* notwithstanding the satisfaction of Christ, and their being under the covert of his Law-magnifying Righteousness.

4*thly*, That, when God is angry with believers for their sins, he pursues them upon the footing of the *Law of Works ;* or, which is the same thing, with the *same anger* wherewith he pursued the Surety, when he was made a curse for them.

5*thly*, That, when God corrects his children, he does it in his *vindictive* or *revenging wrath*, and not in a way of *fatherly chastisement*.

6*thly*, That when a believer *fasts, mourns* for, *confesseth*, and *seeks pardon* of sin ; he is to view himself, *as guilty* of the violation of the *Law of Works*, notwithstanding his being dead to the Law, through faith in Jesus Christ.

SECTION III. Concerning the Obligation of Obedience unto the Law, and the Evangelical Grounds thereof.

HAVING thus essayed to vindicate the *Doctrine of the Grace of God*, from the injuries done to it by the *acts of Assembly* 1720 and 1722 ; and also, the obligation of the holy Law as a *rule of obedience* every where asserted through the foregoing act of Presbytery : Yet, because of the strong propensity of corrupt nature, to turn

G   `the

the grace of God into licentiousnefs; therefore, the Prefbytery judge it expedient to conclude this their *act*, by shewing that the holy Law, as a *Rule of Duty* is still *obligatory* under the gofpel; yea, that the *gofpel* yields *stronger* and more powerful incitements to obedience, than any thing which the *Law* itself, abstractly confidered, can afford.

ARTICLE I.   [Concerning the Obligation of Obedience to the Law.

That the holy Law, as a Rule of Duty is still obligatory under the Gofpel, will appear from several confiderations].   And,

1. This will appear from the *epithets* given unto the Law, under the difpenfation of the gofpel.   Sometimes it is called the Law of Chrift; as in *Gal.* vi. 2. *Bear ye one anothers burdens, and fo fulfil the* LAW OF CHRIST; *John* xiv. 15. *If ye love me, keep MY* COMMANDMENTS; I *Cor.* ix. 21. *Being not without Law to God, but under the* LAW TO CHRIST :   Which expreffions do plainly intimate, that the Law of the *Creator* is now iffued forth to us, in the hand of a *Mediator ;*   and that we, in our obedience, are to eye the authority of God *in him*, becaufe God's name is *in him :*   And indeed, by proclamation from the excellent Glory, we are enjoined to *hear him*, or to receive the Law from *his mouth*, as the great Lawgiver and King whom God hath fet upon his holy hill of *Zion.*   It is agreeably to this, that the Moral Law is called the *Royal Law, James* ii. 8.   For the whole Law, and every article thereof, carries upon it a stamp of the Royal Authority of this King of Saints;   and all the Royal Seed of this great King, have it engraved upon the tables of their hearts, by the power of his Spirit.

2. The Law is given upon *Evangelical*, and, confequently upon *everlafting grounds*, which can never be antiquated or abolifhed; for *Exod.* xx. 1, 2. *God fpake all thefe words, faying, I am the Lord thy God, which have brought thee out of the land of* Egypt, *out of the houfe of bondage.*   It is worthy of notice here, by what arguments the Lord enforces obedience to the Moral Law: The firft is, his *infinite Greatnefs and Immutability ;*   he is the great JEHOVAH, who is being itfelf, and who gives us our being, both in nature and grace;   fo that he has an abfolute fovereignty over us, as the potfherds which his own hand hath made :   But this argument alone is fo awful, that it is ready to difmay and drive us finners away from God;   therefore he next draws us under his fweet and gracious government with *bands of love*, by difplaying himfelf as a God of love, grace and mercy in Chrift, when he adds, I JEHOVAH am THY GOD, in the nearest, fweeteft and strongeft relations.   And this comprehenfive promife, as it is fet in the front of the whole Law;   fo it is annexed to many of the precepts in particular, as in *Levit.* chap. xix.   Obedience to the Law is next enforced,

forced, by the glorious work of *man's redemption* through Jesus Christ, typified by the redemption of *Israel* from their *Egyptian* bondage : And all this our Lesser Catechism well expresseth, in the following words, ' That because God is the Lord, and our God, ' and Redeemer ; therefore we are bound to keep all his com- ' mandments.' So then, the Law of God, as it stands in relation to a Covenant of Grace, being founded upon *gospel grounds*, it must be of *perpetual obligation*. This will further appear, if we consider that,

3. The *end of Christ's coming* was not to destroy the Law but to *fulfil* and *establish* it, Matth. v. 17. He hath fulfilled it as a Cove- nant, by his own personal obedience as our Surety ; and having thus redeemed us from the hands of our enemies, he gives forth the Law, as a *perpetual rule* of obedience to us ; that we, being deliver- ed by him out of the hands of our enemies, might serve him with- out fear, in holiness and righteousness before him, all the days of our life. To the same purpose is that of the Apostle, Rom. iii. 31. *Do we make void the Law through faith? God forbid ; yea, we esta- blish the Law.* It is true indeed, Christ has for ever freed believers from the yoke of the Ceremonial Law ; and also, from the com- manding and condemning power of the Moral Law, as a Covenant, rigorously exacting obedience, as the condition of life, and forbidding sin under the pain of eternal death, without affording strength for o- bedience : Yea, through the grace of the gospel, both our persons and imperfect obedience are accepted in the Beloved. But yet, Christ would not have it so much as enter into the thoughts of any that profess his name, that he came to *dissolve* the obligation of the Law, as a *Rule of Life ;* which appears in the forecited Matth. v. 17. *Think not that I am come to destroy the Law or the Prophets ; I am not come to destroy but to fulfil :* On the contrary, he came to *esta- blish* the obligation of it to the end of the world : For, (says he, verse 18.) *Verily I say unto you, till heaven and earth pass, one jot or one tittle shall in no wise pass from the Law, till all be fulfilled.* And thus he vindicates it from the corrupt glosses of the *Scribes* and *Pharisees*, in his Sermon on the Mount, wherein he discovers its *ob- ligation*, extent and spirituality.

4. Obedience and conformity to the holy Law, is one of the great *ends of our redemption* by Jesus Christ : For *Tit.* ii. 14. *He gave himself for us, that he might redeem us from all iniquity, and purify unto himself a peculiar people, zealous of good works.* And the Apostle *Peter* tells, that Christ hath *redeemed* us from our *vain conversation*, not with silver or gold, or such corruptible things, but with his own precious blood. Wherefore, they dreadfully counter- act the very design of the death of Christ, and of the reign of grace through his righteousness, who imagine that the Doctrine of Grace patronizes a lawless liberty in the way of sin : For Christ died not to procure a liberty *to sin*, but a liberty *from sin :* Accord- ing to *Dan.* ix. 24. *He came to finish the transgression, and to make an end of sins.* 1 John iii. 5. *Ye know that he was manifested to take*

away our *sins.* Verse 6. *Whosoever abideth in him sinneth not: Whosoever sinneth, hath not seen him, neither known him.*

5. All the followers of Jesus Christ are expressly charged to *remember the Law of Moses;* even after the actual rising of the Sun of Righteousness, in his incarnation, and after his saving manifestation in their souls : For it is promised, *Mal.* iv. 2. *But unto you that fear my name shall the Sun of Righteousness arise, with healing in his wings, and ye shall go forth and grow up as calves of the stall :* And then it follows, verse 4. *Remember ye the Law of* Moses *my servant, which I commanded unto him in* Horeb, *for all* Israel. Where, by the Law of *Moses,* we are not to understand the *Ceremonial Law,* which being the shadow of good things to come, did evanish at the exhibition of the Son of God in the flesh : But it is *that* Law of *Moses,* which was published by God on mount *Sinai;* that Law which was written by God's finger on Tables of Stone, and laid up in the Ark, to be preserved there, as a binding Rule of Obedience upon all, unto the end of the world. Such a regard had Christ unto this Law, and the honour of it, that he not only fulfilled the righteousness thereof as a covenant, by his holy obedience ; but in his example, hath left us a *pattern of all gospel-holiness :* And he requires of all who are called by his name, that they depart from iniquity, that they should *follow him,* and be holy *as he is holy ;* and declares that, except their faith in him bring forth the *fruits of obedience* unto his Law, their faith is *dead :* Accordingly, at the last day, their faith in him will be tried by the *fruits* thereof, *Matth.* xxv. 34,—45.

Thus it appears, that the grace of the gospel doth no way *dissolve* the obligation of the Royal Law, as a *Rule of Obedience;* but that on the contrary, it doth *establish* and sweeten the same. Now that which *sweetens* it to believers is, that it is the *Law of Christ;* it is *his* Commandments, and therefore not grievous ; *his* yoke, and therefore easy ; *his* burden, and therefore light. The Law was given by *him* upon mount *Sinai; he* was in the midst of that General Assembly of Angels, convened at the publication of the Law, even *he* who ascended up on high, and led captivity captive : Hence is that expression, *Gal.* iii. 19. *It was ordained by Angels in the hand of a Mediator.* It was ordained by Christ authoritatively, and by Angels ministerially. Christ is the great Mediator, through whose hand the Law is transmitted to us ; and this serves wonderfully to sweeten it : For he not only slays the enmity between God and man ; but he also reconciles the *Law* to *sinners,* and reconciles *sinners* to the *Law.* There is mutual enmity between the Law and every sinner, by nature : The Law accuses, curses and condemns the sinner ; and the sinner is not subject unto the Law, neither indeed can be, because it is opposite unto his lusts.

Now Christ, as he reconciles God and man ; so he reconciles the Law to the sinner, and the sinner to the Law. (1.) He reconciles the *Law* to the *sinner,* that believes in him ; for *against such there is no Law,* Gal. v. 23. Rom. viii. 1. There is no condemning Law no purfuing Law, *Rom.* viii. 32, 33. Though the Law, as it is in the hand of an abfolute God, is an enemy unto the finner out of Chrift, condemning and purfuing him, *Gal.* iii. 10. Yet fo foon as he is in Chrift, it neither condemns nor purfues him, but it becomes a friendly counfellor, to direct him in the way of duty ; and as fuch, it fays, *This is the way walk ye in it.* (2.) As Chrift reconciles the **law** to the finner, fo he reconciles the heart of the *finner* to the *law*, infomuch, that he delights in the law of the Lord, after the inward man ; he efteems all God's Commandments concerning all things, to be right ; and is ready to fay with David, *O how love I thy law !* Pfal. cxix. 97. *Hold up my goings in thy paths, that my footfteps flip not,* Pfal. xvii. 5.

And all this Chrift fweetly effectuates upon the finner in a day of power, by the execution of his feveral offices, as a Prophet, Prieft, and King. As a *Prophet*, he interprets and opens up the law in its purity and fpirituality ; he opens our eyes, to behold wondrous things out of his law. As a *Prieft*, he fatisfies juftice for our fins, covers our obedience, perfumes our fervices, and procures our acceptance by the fweet incenfe of his interceffion. And as a *King*, he tranfmits the Law to his fubjects with the ftamp of *his* authority, as he is the great God our Saviour, and as God is in him a *reconciled* God, proclaiming his name, *The Lord, the Lord God, merciful and gracious, long-fuffering, and abundant in goodnefs and truth.* Exod. xxxiv. 6.

A r t i c l e II. [Concerning the Evangelical grounds of obedience to the Law.]

Thus the Law, in the hand of a Mediator, or as it ftands in fubordination to the grace of the gofpel, is not to be confidered as a rule of acceptance for juftification ; but as a rule of obedience and fanctification : By which obedience we teftify our gratitude, and glorify God. And here,

1. Our obedience to the Law is to proceed upon *evangelical principles.* Now, the leading principle of obedience to the Law, is faith in Jefus Chrift ; hence, all true obedience is called the *obedience of Faith.* The Spirit of life that is in Chrift Jefus, enters into the dead foul, and works faith in it, whereby it is united to Chrift as a Head of influence ; and then the life it lives is *by the faith of the Son of God. I live,* fays *Paul, yet not I, but Chrift liveth in me.* All acts of obedience in believers are acts of the *life of Chrift* in them. All acts of obedience, performed by an unbelieving finner, are but *dead works :* Whereas the believer, having the life and fpirit of Chrift in him, prefents himfelf a *living facrifice* to God, which is our reafonable fervice.

2. Gofpel-obedience to the holy Law, proceeds upon *evangelical motives ;* namely, the confideration of the matchlefs grace, love and mercy of God, manifefted in Chrift. Faith, viewing the excellency of God's loving-kindnefs, the height and depth, the breadth and length whereof paffeth all knowledge ; the foul thereupon cries out,

Lord

Lord, what wilt thou have me to do? What shall I render unto the Lord for all his benefits toward me? As God's love to us moved him to do all that he hath done for us, in the work of redemption; fo, that faith, which worketh by love, makes the foul active to do all for his glory and honour.

3. Gofpel-obedience is influenced by *evangelical affections*, fuch as love, delight, zeal, filial fear, and the like; according as the Apoftle fpeaks, *Gal.* v. 6. *Faith worketh by love.* Faith, as was faid, difcovers the tranfcendent love of God in Chrift: And, as one fire kindles another; fo the love of God, apprehended by faith, both kills the enmity of the heart, and kindles a flame of love there toward God in Chrift, that many waters cannot quench, and all floods are not able to drown; and this love powerfully influences obedience to the holy Law, *If ye love me,* fays Chrift, *keep my commandments.* *Who fhall feparate us,* fays the Apoftle, *from the love of Chrift?* The love of *felf* influences the obedience of the legalift; but the love of *Chrift* conftrains the believer: And this love begets delight, a ready mind, and fervency of fpirit in ferving the Lord, *Pfal.* cxix. 35. *Rom.* xii. 11.

4. Gofpel-obedience is performed to a *Gofpel-end;* which is the honour of Chrift, and the glory of God in him: For God will have all men to honour the Son, even as they honour the Father; and thus it is that, as in *Rom.* xiv. 8. *We live unto the Lord,* doing all to the honour of Chrift, and the glory of God in him. Chrift is called the *Alpha* and *Omega,* the *Firft* and the *Laft;* fo ought he to be unto us, in the whole of our obedience, the Beginning and the Ending of all we do. The unregenerate finner acts *from* himfelf and *for* himfelf, according to *Hof.* x. 1. *Ifrael is an empty vine, he bringeth forth fruit to himfelf: Self* is the firft principle and laft end of all that he doth; and therefore, in all his doings, he is wholly rejected of God. But, with the believer as fuch, *Chrift* is the firft principle of his life of holinefs, and his laft end therein: *He* only muft bear the glory of what he has wrought for us, and of what he works in us or by us, in a way of doing or fuffering, *Rev.* v. 12.

To conclude, As obedience to the holy Law of God, was indifpenfibly required of innocent man; by an obligation neceffarily arifing from the very nature of the Creator and creature, and the effential relation betwixt them: So, mankind having finned, and come fhort of the glory of God, the whole difpenfation of the free grace and love of God through Jefus Chrift, is juft calculate for reftoring fallen man unto a capacity of glorifying God, in time and eternity, by obedience unto the eternal and holy Law: " He hath " chofen us in him, before the foundation of the world, that we " fhould be holy, and without blame before him, in love," *Eph.* i. 4. " Jefus Chrift gave himfelf for us, that he might redeem us " from all iniquity, and purify unto himfelf a peculiar people, " zealous of good works," *Tit.* ii. 13, 14. " Herein is my Father " glorified (fays he, *John* xv. 8.) that ye bear much fruit:" And fo, he muft prefent the Church unto himfelf a " glorious church,
" not

" not having fpot or wrinkle, or any fuch thing," *Eph.* v. 27.
Thus, gofpel-obedience is of fuch importance unto the difpenfation
of grace, that it is a principal end whereunto the fame is effentially
fubfervient, and whereunto it only is effectual: So that, according
to the believer's experience and improvement of the free grace
and love of God in the gofpel; accordingly he will neceffarily,
through the whole aim at, and prefs forward unto a glorifying of
God, by perfect conformity unto his holy Law. But the peculiar
encouragement and accefs we have unto holinefs, under the difpenfation of grace, lies in this; That gofpel-obedience muft be performed, not to *juftify our perfons*, but to *honour, glorify* and *declare
our gratitude* to him who *juftifies us freely* by his grace, through
the redemption that is in Chrift Jefus.

Now, man being at firft married to the Law as a hufband, he
hath a ftrong propenfity to cleave to this hufband, and to feek life
and falvation by doing the works thereof: And it is only the power
of efficacious grace, that can bring a finner to renounce that firft
hufband, and to take on with that new and better hufband, who is
raifed from the dead. Yea, after the foul is actually married to
Chrift, through the remaining *legality* of the heart, it is ready, at
every turn, to caft a fquint look back unto its old hufband, the Law
of Works. Of this the Apoftle complains, *Gal.* iii. 3.—*Having begun in the Spirit, are ye now made perfect by the Flefh ?* that is, do ye
imagine to attain perfection in holinefs or fanctification, by returning
back to the Law, and the Works thereof, for righteoufnefs and life?

There are therefore fundry *legal ends*, that fhould be carefully a-
voided, whether in our *Covenanting*, or in any other acts of obedience : As,

1. We muft not perform the duties of the Law for *righteoufnefs
and juftification ;* for this is to blot out that name of Chrift, *Jer.*
xxiii. 6. The Lord our Righteousness: Nor,

2. To give unto God a *recompence* or *requital* for his mercies.
It is indeed the higheft ingratitude, not to acknowledge him as our
Benefactor, but we can never *recompence* him ; becaufe the creature,
that hath its being and its all from him, can never give any thing
to him but what is his own : *If thou be righteous, what gaveft thou
him, or what receiveth he of thine hand ?* Job. xxxv. 7. And therefore, it well becomes us to acknowledge, when we have done all,
that we are unprofitable fervants, and that our goodnefs extendeth
not unto him.

3. We muft not imagine that, by our acts of obedience, we make
God *amends* for the difhonour done to him by our difobedience ;
nor that thereby we make any *atonement* and *propitiation* for our
fins : For this were to put our obedience in the room of Chrift our
only propitiation.

4. Neither muft we imagine that, by our obedience and duties,
God is *moved to beftow* his mercies upon us : For, whatever God
beftows upon a finner, is of mere grace and mercy, not for any
works of righteoufnefs done by us.

5. We

5. We must not imagine, that our obedience to the Law doth any way *fix our title* to eternal life ; or that it is any *federal, conditional mean*, in order to our *possessing* eternal life. This indeed were to lay another foundation than that which God hath laid in *Zion* : For both 'our *title* to eternal life, and our *actual possession* thereof at the end of the day, do lean wholly upon our union with Christ by a faith of God's operation ; and another foundation can no man lay. All our hopes and expectations of life and salvation, must be founded upon God's Covenant of grace and promise, established in the second *Adam ;* the condition of which was fulfilled by him, the Covenant-head, in his obedience unto the death. Thus, *David* goes into eternity upon this blessed bottom, singing that song, 2 *Sam.* xxiii. 5. *Although my house be not so with God, yet he hath made with me* (viz. in Christ my new Covenant-head) *an everlasting Covenant, ordered in all things and sure : For this is all my salvation, and all my desire.*——Now,

Faith acting upon this Covenant of rich and free grace, has a manifold influence upon our obedience to the Law : Which may be cleared in considering,

A r t i c l e III.　The Connection betwixt *God's Covenant of Grace* and *our Covenant of Duties*, and the influence the *one* has upon the *other*.

The Covenant of Grace which is made with, and stands fast in *Christ* our glorious Head, lays us under much further obligation to duty and service, than the Covenant of Works, even while it stood in the first *Adam*. We are more constrained to obedience under the former, than ever *Adam*, in a state of innocency, was under the latter : And our obligation to vow and pay our vows, to covenant and perform, or keep our Covenants of duty and service to God in Christ, is yet more strengthened and furthered ; by our being under a fuller and clearer dispensation of the Covenant of Grace, than what these had who lived under the Old-Testament, or the dark legal dispensation of this Covenant of Grace. How the obligation is strengthened, and what influence the *Covenant of Grace* hath upon our *Covenants of Duty*, service and obedience, may appear in the following *respects*.

First, In respect of *life ;* which Christ came to give, and to give more abundantly, *John* x. 10. Our life being in the second *Adam*, secured or hid with Christ in God ; the more of this is communicated to us, the more are we in case for lively service, and bound to devote the life that comes to us by the death and life of Christ, unto the obedience of him who died for us ; that we who live should not henceforth live unto ourselves, but unto him who died for us, and rose again, 2 *Cor.* v. 15.

Secondly, In respect of *light* ; which shines more brightly in the gospel. The light of the knowledge of the glory of God in the face of Jesus Christ, given there, to inform the mind, transform the

heart,

heart, and reform the life, 2 *Cor.* iii. 18. obliges us to walk as children of light, *Eph.* v. 8. The more we see in gospel-light, how Christ hath saved us by fulfilling the Law perfectly for us as a Covenant of Works, the more we are constrained to glorify him by our conformity to the Law as a rule of duty and obedience, *Gal.* ii. 19. 20. *Rom.* vii. 4.

Thirdly, In respect of *liberty :* Spiritual liberty, as well as spiritual life and light, is greater and more glorious, by the more plentiful effusion of the Spirit in the gospel-dispensation of the Covenant of Grace, than what we could have had either by the old Covenant of Works, or the old legal dispensation of the new Covenant, 2 *Cor.* iii. 7, 8, 9, 10, 11, 17. If the Son make us free, then are we free indeed, *John* viii. 36. This is a freedom that looses us from sin, and binds us to duty, *Rom.* vi. 17, 18. *Psal.* cxvi. 16.

Fourthly, In respect of *love* and *gratitude*; to which nothing leads us so much, as the display of the grace and love of God to us in the new Covenant. This love kills our enmity and begets love, so that the love of Christ constrains us to his service, 2 *Cor.* v. 14. Being drawn powerfully with bands of love, we run cheerfully the way of his Commandments.

Fifthly, In respect of *joy* ; which the knowledge of the joyful sound of the gospel brings in more plentifully, even joy unspeakable and full of glory. This joy of the Lord is our strength, encouraging us to walk in the light of his countenance, *Psal.* lxxxix. 15, 16, 17. and joyfully to *devote* ourselves and our service to him.

Sixthly, In respect of *hope.* For, as the gospel opens the door of faith, that we may enter into Christ, and close with him for sanctification as well as righteousness ; and so be in case for the duties of holiness outwardly, having the heart purified by faith to the exercise of grace inwardly : So the gospel opens the door of hope, even the hope of heaven and eternal life, at the end of our course of gospel-obedience. By the Gospel of Christ, of his death and resurrection, we are begotten to a lively hope of being like him, by seeing him as he is ; *and every man that hath this hope in him, purifieth himself, even as he is pure,* 1 *John* iii. 2, 3.

Seventhly, In respect of *power,* or divine virtue and efficacy ; whereof especially the gospel-dispensation of the new Covenant is the channel. It is said to be *the power of God unto salvation, to every one that believeth ;—for therein is the righteousness of God revealed from faith to faith, Rom.* i. 16, 17. Thus, as it is the Revelation of Grace reigning through the righteousness of Christ unto eternal life, it is the organ of the power of God unto our salvation ; and so it has not only a moral *argumentative* influence upon holiness, but also a physical and powerful *operative* influence, drawing us with bands of love unto his service, and pulling down the strong holds of sin which stands in opposition thereunto, 2 *Cor.* x. 4, 5.

Eighthly, In respect of the *promise* of the Covenant of Grace ; as it is a Covenant promising all grace, both habitual and actual, *Ezek.* xxxvi. 25, 26, 27. Grace for performing every duty required in

the

the precept of the Law, is given forth to us in the promise of the Gospel : And, as we cannot set about vowing or resolving to perform any duty commanded in the Law, without the grace promised in the Gospel, so the grace here promised, is to be apprehended and depended upon by faith, as the great encouragement to vow and resolve upon obedience, saying with *David*, Psal. cxix. 106. *I have sworn, and I will perform it, that I will keep thy righteous judgments.* As we have here the promise of the Spirit in the plentiful effusion thereof, to make us fruitful in holiness, *Isa.* xliv. 3, 5. the promise of strength, to walk and run in the way of the Lord, *Isa.* xl. 29, 31. the promise of recovery, in case of failures and decays, *Hos.* xiv. 7. the promise of perseverance to the end, in a course of gospel-obedience, *Jer.* xxxii. 40. 1 *Pet.* i. 5. So, having these and the like promises, that by these we may be partakers of the divine nature, we are encouraged to *cleanse ourselves from all filthiness of the flesh and spirit, perfecting holiness in the fear of God,* 2 *Cor.* vii. 1.

Ninthly, In respect of the *authority* enjoining obedience upon us, and calling us to devote ourselves and our service to him. Though this authority is originally the same that enjoined obedience upon man in the first Covenant ; yet it appears to us, in the gospel glass, more amiable and lovely, by its being not the authority of an *absolute God*, but of *God in Christ*, reconciling the world to himself. While God is related unto us, as our God and Redeemer, we are laid under the strongest obligations to duty and obedience ; according to the import of the preface to the Ten Commandments, " That, because God is the Lord, and our God, and Redeemer ; " therefore we are bound to keep all his Commandments."

Tenthly, In respect of the *furniture* we have in our new Covenant-head, the Lord Jesus Christ. Having in him righteousness for acceptance, and strength for assistance, in every duty, and particularly in solemn *vowing* of obedience to him, *Isa.* xliv. 3, 4, 5. the Spirit of all grace being above measure in our glorious Head, for our use and behoof : We are called to be *strong in the grace that is in Christ Jesus*, 2 Tim. ii. 1. to be *strong in the Lord, and in the power of his might*, Eph. vi. 10. by whom strengthening we can do all things, *Phil.* iv. 13. This furniture we have always in him, as our new Covenant-head, and always access to the benefit of it by faith, the proper language whereof is, *Surely in the Lord have I righteousness and strength*, Isa. xlv. 24. And as without this faith, it is impossible to please God by any duty or service ; so by this faith, we are in case to please God, and serve him spiritually and acceptably. There is no comparison between the furniture we once had in the first *Adam*, and this furniture we have in *Christ ;* which is no less than all the fulness of the Godhead dwelling in him, so as we also are *complete in him*, Col. ii. 9, 10. *And of his fulness have all we received, and grace for grace*, John i. 16. according to his promise, *My grace is sufficient for thee ; for my strength is made perfect in weakness*, 2 Cor. xii. 9. As therefore

we

we are called to *work out our own salvation with fear and trembling;
for it is God which worketh in us both to will and to do, of his good
pleasure,* Phil. ii. 12, 13. and to *sanctify ourselves,* because he is the
Lord that *sanctifies us,* Lev. xx. 7, 8. So, as for the great work of
covenanting to serve and obey him, we may with humble confidence set about it, in the faith of this *new Covenant furniture* we
have in Jesus Christ; saying, as it is in *Psal.* lxxi. 16. *I will go
in the strength of the Lord God; I will make mention of thy righteousness, even of thine only.*
Extracted—

JOHN POTTS, *Pr. Cls.*

The following extract from the *Display of the Secession
Testimony*, Vol. I. page 187. may be added here, to
illustrate what is taught concerning the *Appropriation*
of Faith, in the preceeding Act, Sect. 2. Art. 2.

The Associate Presbytery do teach, in their *Act concerning the
Doctrine of Grace,*—that this persuasion is competent to a person,
in the language of justifying faith, *viz.* " Jesus Christ is *mine,* I
" shall have life and salvation by him ; and whatsoever Christ did
" for the redemption of mankind, he did it for *me.*" Thus, faith
immediately terminates upon a *present* special interest in Christ,
Jesus Christ is mine ; as to which, it proceeds upon the present *revelation* and *offer* of him in the gospel, *looking out* to that,—without *looking back* to any divine purposes or intentions : And according to the mysterious order of grace, the Lord gives *truth* to this
special interest, *at the time* of faith's applying Christ to the soul; the
person being actually invested with his justifying righteousness, and
accepted in the sight of God on that account,—which never becomes *true* in the case of any, *till* the moment of believing. In the
next place, it is quite inseparable from the faith of this *special* interest in Christ, and must lie in the same act of faith,—to believe
eternal salvation by Christ ; *I shall have life and salvation by him.*
Now this faith of a *special saving* interest in Christ—must likewise
by the same act, in this due order, terminate upon a special interest
in all his redeeming work ; *whatsoever Christ did for the redemption
of mankind he did it for me.*
As to which last article, we may observe,—that it is entirely
different from a believing, that *Christ intentionally died for the person in particular :* As this faith is the same, upon the matter, with
the faith of *election ;* which, however attainable it be, can noway
belong to faith *as justifying.* But when Christ with his whole salvation is applied by faith, upon the ground of the gospel-offer and
call ; then *whatsoever he did for the redemption of mankind,* doth
therein actually *terminate* upon the person,—and is believed so to
do.

do. Wherefore as to the plea of juftifying faith, [whatfoever Chrift did for the redemption of mankind, he did it *for me*]; the meaning is not, *for me*, by a foregoing *purpofe* and *intention:* But the meaning is, *for me* by a following *iffue* and *termination* thereof upon me ; through the gofpel-offer and call, embraced by faith.

As when a traveller is entertained in a houfe upon his way,—he eats what is fet before him, without any queftion ; juft upon feeing that, in its nature, it is every way *fuitable* and *fufficient* for his need,—and that he is *freely invited* to the ufe thereof. And his very *eating* of the food implies a concluding that all the *preparation* of it was *for him ;* becaufe the preparation of it terminates in him, by the food itfelf doing fo : Which yet is entirely different from his being otherwife informed and believing,—that the food was *intentionally* provided and made ready for him, before he faw it.

www.ingramcontent.com/pod-product-compliance
Lightning Source LLC
Chambersburg PA
CBHW021512090426
42739CB00007B/577